Personnel Law Answer Book

1991 Supplement

James O. Castagnera, Esq.
Saul, Ewing, Remick & Saul

THE PANEL ANSWER BOOK SERIES

Library of Congress Cataloging-in-Publication Data

Castagnera, James.
Personnel law answer book. 1991 supplement / James O. Castagnera.
p. cm.
ISBN 1-878375-25-3
1. Labor Laws and legislation—United States—Miscellanea.
I. Castagnera, James. Personnel law answer book. II. Title.
KF3319.3.C37 1991 Suppl.
344.73'01--dc20
[347.3041] 89-25482
CIP

ISBN 1-878375-25-3

by
PANEL PUBLISHERS, INC.
A Wolters Kluwer Company
36 West 44th Street
New York, NY 10036
(212) 790-2000
Customer Service: (212) 790-2090

Printed in the United States of America

How to Use the 1991 Supplement

This Supplement brings your *Personnel Law Answer Book* up to date with current law and regulations. It includes (1) an introduction, (2) a list of new and revised questions, (3) new and revised questions and answers for each chapter in the base volume, (4) a new chapter on government contractors, (5) a revised appendix and new appendix on recent and pending legislation, and (6) a cumulative index.

Most of the questions and answers in this supplement are new; in some instances, old questions have been rewritten to reflect recent changes in the law or legal climate.

The appendices on recent and pending legislation update the status of all the bills mentioned in Appendix A to the base volume and also list important new legislative initiatives. When pending legislation has become law (for example, Plant Closing legislation), questions and answers about the new law appear in the appropriate chapter (for example, Employment Termination).

The revised questions and answers in this supplement are identified by the numbers used in the original volume. New questions have been added in the appropriate sequence and are indicated by a point number (e.g., 12.1, 12.2, 12.3, etc.).

The cumulative index references the material in both the original work and this supplement. *This index replaces the index in the original volume.* If the reference in the index is to a question number that includes an "**S**" (e.g., 12**S**), the information is in the supplement, not the original volume. References without an "**S**" notation are to questions that appear in the original volume.

This volume is a cumulative supplement, incorporating and updating all appropriate questions and answers from the *1990 Supplement*. Consequently, subscribers should discard last year's Supplement and retain the original (main) volume and this *1991 Supplement*.

About the Author

JAMES O. CASTAGNERA is a labor lawyer with Saul, Ewing, Remick & Saul, a Philadelphia firm of nearly 200 lawyers with offices in Washington, D.C., Wilmington, Delaware, and elsewhere. He has authored several books, including the main volume of *Personnel Law Answer Book* and *How to Prepare an Employee Handbook* for Panel Publishers. He holds his J.D. and Ph.D. from Case Western Reserve University and has taught law at the University of Texas in Austin.

About Panel Publishers, Inc.

Panel Publishers derives its name from a panel of business professionals who organized in 1964 to publish authoritative, timely books, information services, and journals written by specialists to assist accountants, tax practitioners, attorneys, and other business professionals; human resources, compensation and benefits, and pension and profit-sharing professionals; and owners of small to medium-sized businesses. Our mission is to provide practical, solution-based "how-to" information to business professionals.

Also available in the Panel Answer Book series:

Health Insurance Answer Book
The Pension Answer Book
Nonqualified Deferred Compensation Answer Book
The S Corporation Answer Book
Employee Benefits Answer Book
Employee Assistance Law Answer Book

To order or for more information,
contact Panel Publishers, Inc.
36 W. 44th Street, New York, NY 10036
or call (212) 790-2090

The following editorial and production professionals have contributed to the publication of this book: Publisher, Richard H. Kravitz, CPA; Vice President, Editorial, Richard D. Walker, CPA; Director, New Product Development, Mark D. Persons, Esq.; Executive Editor, Isabelle Cohen; Production Manager, Jan Lavin; and Assistant Production Manager, Carol Biedrzycki.

PANEL PUBLISHERS, INC.
Practical Solutions for Business Professionals

Table of Contents

Introduction

A quarter century has passed since the 1964 Civil Rights Act was enacted, starting a long line of labor legislation. The Equal Pay Act, the Age Discrimination in Employment Act (ADEA), the Occupational Safety and Health Act (OSHA), and the Employee Retirement Income Security Act (ERISA)—one by one, the laws marched forth from Capitol Hill to be joined at various state lines by proliferating state and local legislation. State and federal courts began reexamining and redefining key (often long-settled) areas of the common law: employment at will, wrongful termination, intentional infliction of emotional distress, defamation, negligent maintenance of a workplace. The latest in this long line of legislation is the American with Disabilities Act [ADA], signed by President George Bush on July 26, 1990. See Appendix C for a full description and explanation of the ADA.

Equally important is that the rate of change in labor and employment law seems to be ever accelerating.

To help you cope with the rush of events, and to keep the main volume current, we have put together this cumulative supplement. In it, we track changes in the subjects covered in the *Personnel Law Answer Book* main volume. We also pick up new topics that were not ripe for discussion in the original work.

In general, 1990 was not a precedent-setting year for labor and employment law in the same magnitude as the year before. While the Americans with Disabilities Act became law, the long-anticipated federal family leave law languished in the face of a threatened presidential veto. On the labor management front, unions seem to be continuing their long slide toward a membership nadir that has not yet been fathomed.

On the other hand, there have been substantial expansion of lawsuits involving employee misappropriation of trade secrets, breach of noncompetition agreements, and similar unfair trade practices by former employees. Perhaps this litigation is just one more symptom of the post-industrial era, or the "Information Age;" the *knowledge* of an employee is now a more valuable asset of the company than the property, plant, and equipment.

Indeed, human resources have clearly become the key components of a competitive business, just as land was paramount in the days when agriculture was our leading industry and as capital equipment became after the Industrial Revolution. In fact, Professor Harry C. Katz of the Cornell Institute of Collective Bargaining has pointed out that the human resources director's office has moved from the far end of the executive suite to the space adjacent to the plant manager's office in many companies. Enlightened corporations may have moved ahead of Congress during the past year regarding workers' family leave and other quality-of-life issues. Instead of driving change, the law may lag behind corporate actions throughout the 1990s. Astute business people do not need laws to tell them that good human resources policies and practices are essential to success in the Information Age.

James O. Castagnera, Esq.
December 1990

Listing of Questions

The Employer-Employee Relationship

Hiring and Evaluating Employees

Coping With Labor Unions

Employment Discrimination

The Immigration Reform and Control Act of 1986

Employee Compensation

Employee Fringe Benefits

Executive Compensation

Job Safety

Employment Termination

Government Contractors

The Employer-Employee Relationship

Q. 1 What constitutes an employer-employee relationship?

Generally, an employer-employee relationship is created as a result of the terms of an agreement (contract), either oral or written, or is implied by the courts because of the parties' conduct. When the employer-employee relationship is not defined by either an oral or written agreement, that relationship is said to be one of "employment at will." Employment at will is a rule or presumption that is created by courts to govern the relationship between employer and employee when there is no other discernible standard. The courts created this construct so that, unless an employer and employee agreed upon employment for a fixed period, the employment was at will, and therefore could be terminated by either party without any advance notice or reason.

An individual can, and usually does, become an employee by virtue of some agreement or by virtue of the sheer status of employment. This, however, is distinguishable from the legal relationships between those persons who have a possessory or "equity" interest in the company.

The trend in the past two decades has been away from collective security (i.e., labor unions) and toward a return to individual employment relationships. Legislators and courts have recognized this by giving employees, as individuals, more and more security and protection. The traditional concept of employment at will has been the target of ever-increasing restrictions during the past 20 years or so.

Although there is considerable concern among employees that their rights be clearly articulated in written contracts, employees may still possess a contractual relationship with their employers even if it is not reduced to writing.

Q.3 Does employment at will survive today?

Employment at will seems to be alive and well. The strongest indication of this survival comes from the National Conference of Commissioners on Uniform State Laws, the prestigious group that drafts and supports uniform acts across the entire spectrum of American law and jurisprudence. They have most recently drafted a Uniform Employment Termination Act for the 50 states to consider enacting. The proposed act permits employers to discharge employees, provided there is an individually-executed employment agreement which guarantees a minimum schedule of graduated severance payments. If this law were violated by a wrongful discharge, the employee suing under it could get back pay and attorney fees, but no compensatory, e.g., pain and suffering, or punitive (punishment) damages. The Uniform Act, if adopted by a state as written, would also disallow "add-on" counts in a wrongful discharge action for such popular claims as defamation and intentional infliction of emotional distress. Although the uniform act does bring severance pay into play, it is, on balance, a conservative measure that would benefit *businesses* in many states, whereas the current court-mode law may be much more pro-employee.

Q. 3.1 What legislation restricts or modifies the employment-at-will doctrine?

Since the Depression and the New Deal, federal law has added an increasing number of restrictions on employers' ability to fire and hire people at will. The restrictions that Congress has placed upon employers are numerous and affect who can be hired, the environment in which employees work, how an employee can be terminated, and the right of the employee to ensure that his or her employer complies with state and federal law.

The Civil Rights Act of 1964 (which bans discrimination on the basis of race, sex, color, religion, or national origin) is a well-known and common example of the impact of such laws. Other well-known laws that embody these changes in the employer-employee relationship include statutes protecting the aged, minorities, whistleblowers, women, union members, and those employees seeking to improve working conditions. Many states have enacted similar statutes to keep pace with, and in some instances exceed, the federal laws in these areas.

Other laws restricting employment at will include the Comprehensive Environmental Response, Compensation and Liability Act (CERCLA), which prohibits employers from discriminating against or otherwise penalizing an employee who provides information to the state or federal government pertaining to his or her employer's disposal or handling of toxic substances; the Age Discrimination in Employment Act of 1967 (ADEA); the Fair Labor Standards Act (FLSA); the National Labor Relations Act (NLRA); and the Occupational Safety and Health Act (OSHA), to name a few.

Q. 3.2 What other legislation protects employees at work?

In addition to those statutes that prohibit discrimination against employees on the basis of race, age, gender, or other immutable characteristics, there is a wide body of legislation that protects employees while working for the employer. For example, OSHA created a vast body of regulations and procedures to ensure that the occupational hazards associated with various types of employment and the machinery used by various employees is maintained in such a way that the safety of the employees is not compromised needlessly.

A recent example of OSHA's continuing involvement in employee safety is the nationwide comprehensive study of the extent and types of injuries associated with supermarket laser scanners. Another less visible effort includes the recent House subcommittee's hearing on the source of the toxic substances that caused an explosion that killed six firefighters in Kansas City, Missouri. These examples evidence the breadth and scope of federal intervention in all aspects of employer-employee relations, including the at-will arena. Other well-known examples of this type of legislation include the Longshoremen's and Harbor Workers Compensation Act, the Mine Safety and Health Act of 1977, the Railroad Safety Act, and the Surface Mining Control and Reclamation Act.

Finally, there are numerous other statutes that influence and sometimes dictate an employer's conduct. For example, the Immigration Reform and Control Act of 1986 (IRCA) imposes penalties for the employment of illegal aliens. Although the purposes of IRCA are manifold, one of its obvious purposes is to establish limitations on whom an employer can hire. (See Questions 256–282 in the main volume.)

Q. 3.3 What are "whistleblower" laws?

Both federal and state legislatures have restricted the traditional employment-at-will rule when public health, safety, or ethics in government is involved. The legislation is intended to provide protection for employees who report their employer's statutory violations to appropriate governmental agencies or authorities. Whistleblower protection is generally limited to good-faith reports of suspected violations.

Q. 3.4 What are the provisions of federal whistleblower laws?

A number of federal statutes (e.g., ADEA) protecting civil service employees prohibit the government from taking any action against an employee who discloses information he or she reasonably believes reveals a violation of law, mismanagement, waste of funds, abuse of authority, or a substantial and specific duty to public safety and health.

On April 10, 1989, the Whistleblower Protection Act of 1989 was enacted. The Act is designed to protect federal employees from reprisals resulting from whistleblowing on waste, fraud, and unnecessary government expenditures. The Act establishes a Special Counsel's office to act in the interests of these employees.

Q. 3.5 What must a federal employee show to prevail in a claim of wrongful discharge under the federal whistleblower acts?

The employee must establish that:

(1) A protected disclosure was made;

(2) The accused official knew of the disclosure;

(3) Retaliation resulted; and

(4) There is a connection between the retaliation and the employee's discharge.

Q. 3.6 Do the federal whistleblower laws preempt state law claims?

In June 1989, the U.S. Supreme Court unanimously held that Section 210 of the Energy Reorganization Act—the Act's whistleblower provision—does *not* preempt a state law claim of intentional infliction of emotional distress by a worker in the nuclear power industry. Two lower courts had previously dismissed the lawsuit of a former General Electric employee who claimed she had been transferred, harassed, and finally, fired because of her complaint to the Nuclear Regulatory Commission about alleged inadequate clean-up efforts at a nuclear fuel processing plant in Wilmington, NC. Writing for the full Court, Justice Blackman stated that Congress never intended to preempt all state law remedies when it enacted nuclear safety regulations. The high Court held that there was no irreconcilable conflict between Section 210 and a state-law tort claim for harassment.

Q. 18.1 What purposes do written employment contracts serve?

In addition to specifying the expectations of both the employer and employee, in terms of both tasks and compensation, such agreements also provide for termination policies, buy-out provisions, covenants not to compete, confidentiality agreements, choice of law provisions, and other concerns that are particular to specific employers' practices or professions.

Q. 18.2 What are the limitations of a written employment contract?

While employment agreements can define each party's rights and responsibilities, they can also establish an employer's intention or course of conduct that is not apparent on the face of the document—that is, is not explicitly spelled out in writing. Indeed, the use of such agreements and, to an increasing extent, employee handbooks has left some employers in the precarious position of responding to disgruntled employees' claims to rights that were never embodied in the parties' contractual relationship. These employee rights, however, have become binding upon the employer because of the larger picture that is created when the employment agreement is read together with various office memoranda or other corporate documents. It is therefore crucial that all such documents be carefully drafted. The commitment to precision and clarity must include the terms and conditions that are to be subject to the agreement and those terms that are clearly excluded from the document. The tendency toward over-inclusion is a shortcoming that frequently arises with ill-considered or hasty draftsmanship.

Q. 22.1 Can employment agreements be modified?

Yes. Indeed, it is because such agreements can be modified that employers are sometimes held accountable for consequences far beyond those considered at the time the various agreements were drafted. On the other hand, bad employment agreements can be modified and improved upon. However, as with any contract, the employer must secure the agreement of the other party for the agreement to be contractually binding. Although the reformation may be initially costly, it can serve an employer's long-term interest to reduce its ongoing liability by creating inducements for an employee to renegotiate an existing contract. This ebb and flow in employer-employee negotiations is most notable in union-management contract negotiations.

Q. 23.1 Are arbitration clauses in individual employment contracts enforceable?

Under the Federal Arbitration Act (9 U.S.C. §§1–15) and many analogous state arbitration acts, arbitration clauses are fully enforceable. Thus, (1) a party to such an employment contract can get a court order to compel the other party to submit to arbitration, and (2) the victorious party can sue to enforce the arbitrator's award against a recalcitrant opponent.

Q. 23.2 Which employment contracts are covered by the Federal Arbitration Act?

As a general rule, all employment contracts involving companies engaged in interstate commerce are subject to the jurisdiction of the Federal Arbitration Act. Under a long series of Supreme Court decisions dating back to the New Deal era, most commercial and industrial activities are considered to be involved in interstate commerce.

Q. 23.3 Are there any employment contracts not covered by the Federal Arbitration Act?

Employment contracts involving workers who are directly engaged in transportation—seamen, railroad workers, airline employees—are expressly exempt from the Federal Arbitration Act. Additionally, there may be a few businesses so local in nature that they can successfully show they are not in the flow of interstate commerce. Moreover, when the arbitration agreement expressly provides that the laws of the state will govern the agreement, the state law of arbitration applies.

Q. 23.4 Who decides whether or not an employment issue is arbitrable?

Sometimes one party to an employment contract that contains an arbitration clause will claim that the particular dispute is not arbitrable. For example, an employer may want to arbitrate a disagreement involving a collateral agreement outside the four corners of the employment contract (e.g., a supplemental agreement on bonuses or commissions, or a provision in the employee handbook). The employee may argue that his or her agreement to arbitrate does not include disputes not expressly covered in the agreement. Generally, the arbitrator decides the arbitrability issue before reaching the merits of the controversy. Consequently, if the employer files a lawsuit seeking an order to compel the employee to submit to arbitration, the court should limit its inquiry to whether the arbitration clause might arguably apply. If it does apply, jurisdiction should be turned over to the arbitrator to settle the arbitrability issue.

Q. 23.5 What is the standard for determining arbitrability?

There is no statutory definition of arbitrability that applies to all situations. (If there were, the courts, instead of the arbitrators, would most likely decide arbitrability.) Rather, the intent of the contracting parties controls in the question of arbitrability. When the written agreement is ambiguous, the arbitrator must look at other evidence of the parties' intentions at the time they executed the arbitration agreement. This evidence may include other documents, such as letters and memoranda; past practice of the parties; industry customs; reported arbitration awards interpreting the same or similar agreements; and the oral testimony of the employer and the employee.

Q. 23.6 Is an arbitration agreement in an employment contract with a foreign corporation enforceable in the United States?

If a foreign employer enters an employment agreement with an employee in the United States, the company will probably be subject to the same rules as a domestic corporation, including amenability to a suit to compel arbitration. The issue becomes cloudy when the U.S. citizen is employed overseas. It becomes cloudier when the company is owned by a foreign government (see 9 U.S.C., §201 *et seq.*).

Q. 23.7 Are there any alternatives to arbitration to settle employee disputes?

Yes. Some companies have initiated a peer grievance review system. This system originated at a General Electric plant in Maryland and has been found to be very effective.

Studies of the Maryland peer review procedure used at General Electric show that the decisions have varied little from those resulting from a traditional kind of grievance system. However, the employees interviewed explained that they felt they received fairer treatment under the peer review system.

Q. 23.8 What is a "peer grievance review system"?

As instituted in a number of companies, the system consists of a panel of five members frequently chosen as follows: Two members are management (one of which is usually an employee relations manager) and three are nonmanagement or peers. The panel members are volunteers who have been trained in the process of dispute resolution, including legal and ethical considerations. Two peer members are chosen at random by the grievant by pulling names out of a box. The two management members and the two randomly selected peers choose the fifth member, who chairs the panel.

Q. 23.9 What are the steps in the grievance procedure?

The steps in a grievance procedure are:

(1) The individual employee presents the claim to his or her supervisor.

(2) A higher management level reviews the written grievance.

(3) The employee may submit his or her grievance to the peer grievance review panel.

The grievant can receive assistance from someone in the employee relations group or represent himself or herself. Individual grievants may present their disputes, provide comments, and call witnesses before the panel.

The supervisor then presents his or her side of the situation. The panel is free to ask questions or call any witnesses if it chooses to hear additional information.

The panel's decision is by secret ballot. The decision is final, put in writing, and becomes binding on all of the parties. The system applies to all employees, including managers.

All participants agree to confidentiality.

Q. 24 How can employees be prevented from leaving the company and competing against it?

One way to diminish the employee's desire to terminate employment prematurely, and to minimize the damage if he or she does, is to include one or more provisions limiting the employee's ability to use the company's expertise to compete against it. A *covenant not to compete* is a promise that, during the employee's tenure with the company and for a reasonable time afterwards, he or she will not engage in any activities that compete for business against the enterprise. A *confidentiality agreement* states that the employee will keep the firm's proprietary information secret; this usually includes customer lists, trade secrets, and financial information of the company.

As with confidentiality agreements, such restrictions are frowned upon by courts when they go too far. Thus, the courts have increasingly held that the geographical scope and the duration of such agreements are the critical factors that affect, and largely determine, the enforceability of a covenant not to compete.

Q. 25.1 How likely are the courts to enforce confidentiality agreements that employers require employees to execute?

Depending upon the scope, purpose, and duration of such agreements, an employer can compel its employees to maintain the confidentiality of the subject matter of their employment. However, the employer should exercise care in the scope of the restrictions. For example, the courts would not enforce an agreement that prohibits employees from ever disclosing the type of employment they engaged in. The point to always keep in mind is that such agreements should be narrowly tailored to effectuate the employer's legitimately defensible concern. Thus, for example, a car manufacturer need not compel its employees to conceal the fact that they work in an automobile factory. However, the employer would be within its rights to compel its employees not to disclose the design specifications of its vehicles or the particular marketing strategies that the company has developed. Agreements that protect these types of concerns will find favorable protection from the courts.

Q. 32.1 Can a written disciplinary policy alter the at-will relationship?

An employer's written disciplinary policy has been held to have created an implied contract that employees would be fired only for good cause. An employee, therefore, had the right to expect that, in light of his or her satisfactory performance evaluations and the absence of any rule violations, he or she would not be fired. (See Questions 89, 98–105, and 609–616 in the main volume.)

Q. 33 Can an employer create implied contractual terms with an employee handbook?

Yes. Courts will often look to the terms and reasonable expectations that an employee would be likely to draw from a review of the manual. Although a number of factors could affect the court's analysis, the representations contained in such a manual could be construed as elements on which an employee reasonably relied in accepting or continuing employment at a given company. However, such a handbook can also be used to clearly spell out the rights and responsibilities of both the employer and employee. However, as is true of any intention committed to writing, a personnel manual is susceptible to multiple interpretations and possible manipulation or exploitation. Accordingly, employers should always use great care when drafting such documents.

Q. 33.1 What guidelines can an employer follow to avoid lawsuits stemming from disputes over the terms of employment stated or implied by an employee handbook?

An employer should:

(1) Avoid making promises about career opportunities, future compensation, or expected job duties.

(2) Use disclaimers, such as "unless our plans change" or "if we continue to do as well as we have in the past," if promises are made.

(3) Describe benefits using words such as "currently," "at present," or "now," and note that plans are "subject to change."

(4) Include in the personnel manual or employee handbook the statement that employment is "at will" and that "the employee or employer may terminate the employment at any time, and no oral or written promises regarding any terms or conditions of employment can be made, or should be relied upon, except for those made in writing by a designated officer of the organization."

Hiring and Evaluating Employees

Q. 57 Are questions concerning criminal records acceptable?

This is a controversial subject—the Equal Employment Opportunity Commission and other discrimination agencies feel that because members of minority groups are more likely to have arrest records, such questioning has an adverse impact on minorities as a class. A question limited to only convictions is safe, and such inquiries are safer still if (a) the applicant, if hired, will handle money, drugs, or valuables, and (b) only crimes of violence or dishonesty will disqualify the applicant.

The law tends to distinguish between questions about arrests and queries concerning convictions. An arrest is not proof of guilt; perhaps no charges were brought or the applicant was ultimately acquitted. In either case, the applicant does not deserve to be stigmatized. Therefore, it is more appropriate to limit an inquiry to convictions for crimes that indicate unsuitability for the job to be filled.

Q. 57.1 What is "negligent hiring"?

Lawsuits have been brought by victims of criminal, violent, or negligent acts perpetrated by employees whom the employer should not have either hired or retained.

Q. 57.2 What is the best way for employers to avoid negligent hiring suits?

The goal is to avoid hiring the wrong employees in the first place. An employer should examine its screening procedure to see whether it provides a thorough look at an applicant's suitability for employment.

Q. 57.3 What tests do courts use to determine whether an employer has acted negligently in a hiring decision?

The employer must satisfy the court that a reasonable investigation of the employee's background was conducted vis à vis the job for which the employee was hired. Employers should evaluate this information with regard to the possible risk of harm or injury to co-workers or third parties that could result from the conduct of an unfit employee.

Q. 57.4 What are some effective ways to recognize and avoid hiring unfit workers?

Employers should:

(1) Inspect the information an applicant provides for gaps in employment and other suspicious or unusual entries or omissions.

(2) Obtain the applicant's consent to get information from past employers, personal references, and other sources, as well as a waiver and release from liability in connection with the reference check.

(3) Document efforts to obtain information from each previous source, especially if pertinent information was not obtainable from these sources.

(4) Decide whether any information provided by the applicant or learned from previous employers, personal references, or the job interview calls for a criminal record search.

(5) Advise applicants that employment is contingent on a satisfactory reference check.

Q. 57.5 How hard is it to get adequate references from former employers?

Many companies, concerned about defamation lawsuits by former employees, have adopted a policy of responding to reference checks with only the former employee's dates of employment and position held. The author recommends that employers provide only this factual data. Apparently this practice has become so pervasive that, according to some attorneys quoted by the Bureau of National Affairs in its *Daily Labor Report* of May 3, 1990, it is nearly impossible for companies to get adequate referrals on job applicants. Yet, according to the *Daily Labor Report*, few lawsuits—such as libel, slander and invasion of privacy—have resulted from more candid reference replies. A firm's reference policy will depend on many factors, including (1) the applicable state's law of defamation, e.g., whether a qualified business privilege is applied to reference checks, (2) the need for *quid pro quo* referrals from frequently contacted companies, and (3) the reliability of the company's personnel who will respond to such calls.

Q. 61.1 Can a company deny employment on the basis of a credit report?

In addition to the adverse impact issue, employers must consider the Fair Credit Reporting Act. Although this law is better known for its impact on retail sales and credit cards, there are also sections that deal with background investigations of employment applicants. If an employer denies employment to an applicant on the basis of a credit report prepared by a consumer reporting agency, the employer must advise the applicant of the report's existence and that it was the reason for denying employment.

Q. 62.1 What are the requirements of the federal polygraph law?

The Employee Polygraph Protection Act of 1988 prevents most private employers from using lie detector tests to screen job applicants or to test current employees. An employer may use such a test only if it reasonably suspects that an employee was involved in a workplace theft or other incident that caused economic loss to the employer.

Highlights of the Polygraph Protection Act are:

- The law permits private security firms and drug companies to continue to administer lie detector tests to job applicants and employees.
- Federal, state, and local government employers are exempt from the ban and the federal government is allowed to test private consultants or experts under a national security exemption.
- Employers are prohibited from disciplining, discharging, discriminating against, or denying employment or promotions to prospective or current workers solely on the basis of lie detector test results. Employers may request that an employee submit to a lie detector exam during an investigation of a workplace theft or other incident that causes *economic loss or injury* to the employer if (1) the employee had access to the property under investigation, (2) the employer has a *reasonable suspicion* the employee was involved, and (3) the employer provides the employee with a written statement giving its reasons for testing particular employees.
- The law authorizes the Secretary of Labor as well as employees and job applicants to bring civil suits under the Act, and federal courts are given the power to award legal and equitable relief. The Department of Labor may seek civil fines of up to $10,000 against employers that violate the law.
- The law prescribes detailed procedures employers must follow during any permitted lie detector tests.
- The law *does not preempt* any state or local laws or collective bargaining agreements that prohibit lie detector tests or are more restrictive with respect to lie detector tests than the federal law.

Q. 62.2 What is a "lie detector"?

Lie detectors include polygraphs, deceptographs, voice stress analyzers, psychological stress evaluators, or any other similar device that is used for the purpose of rendering a diagnostic opinion regarding an applicant's or employee's honesty.

Q. 62.3 Is anything excluded from the definition of a lie detector?

Yes. Medical tests used to evaluate the presence of controlled substances are excluded. Also excluded are written or oral tests commonly referred to as "honesty" or "paper-and-pencil" tests.

Q. 62.4 What is a "polygraph"?

A polygraph is a device that continuously, visually, permanently, and simultaneously records changes in cardiovascular, respiratory, and electrodermal (electric charges on the skin) patterns. The results of the test are used for rendering a diagnostic opinion regarding a person's honesty.

Q. 62.5 Are the employers *exempt* from the polygraph and lie detector testing prohibitions?

An employer authorized to manufacture, distribute, or dispense a controlled substance may administer a lie detector test to any applicant who would have direct access to the manufacturing, storage, distribution, or sale of any such substances. This exemption does not apply to employers involved in the transportation or storage of these substances. Private employers that provide security and security-related services may test applicants for employment.

Q. 62.6 What are considered employers that provide "security services"?

To be a security service employer, the employer's primary business (more than 50% of annual dollar income) must consist of providing armored car personnel; personnel engaged in the design, installation, and maintenance of security alarm systems; or other uniformed or plainclothes security personnel if their responsibilities include the protection of certain facilities, materials, operations, and assets.

Q. 62.7 What facilities, materials, operations, and assets are Polygraph Protection Act exemptions?

Security services must protect operations, whether privately or publicly owned, that involve a significant impact on the health and safety of any state or its political subdivisions, or on the national security of the United States such as:

- Facilities engaged in the production, transmission, or distribution of electric or nuclear power.
- Public water supply facilities.
- Facilities that ship or store radioactive or other toxic waste materials.
- Public transportation operations.
- Operations that provide currency and securities.
- Communication facilities.
- Hospitals and health research facilities.
- Facilities at which large public events are held.

Q. 62.8 What constitutes an "economic injury" or "loss"?

An economic injury or loss to an employer's business includes theft, embezzlement, misappropriation, or an act of unlawful industrial espionage or sabotage. Unintentional economic losses, such as injury resulting from a workplace accident, do not justify lie detector testing.

Q. 62.9 Can an employer use the polygraph test when thefts are committed by one employee against another employee?

No. The economic loss must be suffered by the employer, not its employees.

Q. 62.10 What constitutes "access to property"?

Access means more than direct physical contact; it includes the opportunity to cause or aid in causing an economic loss or injury. For example, when an employee has the combination to a safe or the ability to falsify records to effectively conceal a loss, he or she has access to property.

Q. 62.11 What constitutes "property"?

Property includes not only tangible items, but also other objects of value, such as technical information, trade secrets, and security codes.

Q. 62.12 What "reasonable suspicion" justifies a lie detector test?

An employer's "reasonable suspicion" must have some observable, articulative basis in fact. Access alone is insufficient to establish reasonable suspicion. It is the employer's burden to establish that reasonable suspicion existed to justify the lie detector examination.

Q. 62.13 What information must an employer provide to an employee prior to giving the examination?

The employer must provide a statement that sets forth with particularity the specific activity or event under investigation. The employer must also reveal the basis for testing a particular employee. This written statement must be signed by a person employed by the company who is authorized to legally bind the employer.

The statement must set forth the *economic loss or injury* suffered by the employer and must indicate that the employee had *access* to the property that is the subject of the investigation. The employer must also describe the basis of its reasonable suspicion.

Q. 62.14 When must this statement be given to the employee who will be tested?

This statement must be given to the employee 48 hours prior to the scheduled examination.

Q. 62.15 Must the statement identify any person(s) who provided the employer with information giving rise to its reasonable suspicion?

No. The employer does not have to reveal the names or identities of co-workers or others who provided information.

Q. 62.16 Who is considered to be an applicant for employment?

An applicant includes not only a person being considered for employment for the first time, but also a current employee who holds a job that is *not* covered by an exception to the Polygraph Protection Act, but who is applying, or is otherwise being considered, for a job that is covered by an exception.

Q. 62.17 What adverse action can an employer take against an employee on the basis of the lie detector test result?

An employer may take adverse action against an employee only with respect to the *prospective* position applied for, not the *current* position the employee holds. For example, an employee attempting to transfer into a security-related position may be denied the transfer if he or she fails a lie detector test, but the test results cannot be used against that person's current employment status.

Q. 62.18 Must the employer's adverse action be founded on something in addition to the lie detector test result?

Yes. An employer's adverse action cannot be based solely on the results of, or the refusal to take, a lie detector test. The action must also be based on either the employee's statements or admissions, or some bona fide reason, such as the employee's employment history.

Q. 62.19 Does the Polygraph Protection Act supersede state or local laws or collective bargaining agreements?

The Polygraph Protection Act does not preempt any provision of state or local law or collective bargaining agreements that either prohibits lie detector tests altogether or is more restrictive with respect to such tests than the Polygraph Protection Act.

Q. 62.20 May an employer ask its employees to waive their rights under the Polygraph Protection Act?

Applicants or employees may not waive any of the rights provided by the Polygraph Protection Act, voluntarily or by contract, unless a specific action or complaint is involved.

Q. 62.21 Are there questions that cannot be asked during a lie detector examination?

Yes. Questions concerning the following are prohibited:

(1) Racial matters;

(2) Religious beliefs;

(3) Political beliefs;

(4) Sexual preferences; or

(5) Union affiliation.

Q. 62.22 Are there regulations regarding the length and frequency of the lie detector test?

Yes. A lie detector test will violate the Polygraph Protection Act if one examiner conducts more than five tests in one day and if each test does not last at least 90 minutes.

Q. 62.23 What types of legal claims can arise from lie detector testing?

Employees have relied on several successful theories to bring lawsuits relating to lie detector testing:

(1) *Public Policy Tort Theory:* Some states have recognized a cause of action when a statute prohibits submitting an employee to a lie detector as a term or condition of employment.

(2) *Breach of Contract:* If the employment relationship is governed by an implied contract not to discharge except for "just cause," the employee may argue that discharge in reliance on the results of a lie detector examination cannot establish "cause."

(3) *Invasion of Privacy:* The constitutions of several states deal with privacy and may apply to the private sector.

(4) *Defamation:* A discharge shortly after a lie detector exam could lead co-workers to infer that the employee was terminated because he or she lied, resulting in the publication of a defamatory statement in the workplace. Under the doctrine of compelled self-publication, an employer's liability may extend to instances in which when seeking employment, the reason for discharge given by a former employee implicated failing a lie detector test.

(5) *Negligence:* If an employee can prove that the exam is not up to industry standards, the examiner's negligence can be imputed back to the employer.

(6) *Intentional Infliction of Emotional Distress:* The issue in this type of litigation is whether the employer's conduct was outside the bounds of "civilized society."

(7) *Discrimination:* Employees have made claims that lie detector tests disproportionately fail blacks because of physiological particularities. Other potential claims include sexual discrimination or sexual harassment based on the polygraph examiner's conduct or offensive questions about sexual preferences and practices.

Q. 62.24 What is "negligent administration" of a lie detector test?

Some courts have recognized a duty to administer the lie detector examination with "due care." Failure to administer the lie detector test with appropriate due care may be the basis for a suit based on negligent administration of a lie detector test. An employee may challenge the examination by claiming that a different examiner would have phrased the questions more clearly, interpreted the chart more skillfully, or taken more time. The statutory standard requires a test to last at least 90 minutes. Shorter examinations may be faulted on their length alone.

Q. 62.25 Can an employee sue his or her employer for negligent administration of a lie detector test?

Yes. Although it is not a common cause of action, several courts have recognized claims by employees for negligent administration of a lie detector test. Considering the recent legislation regarding restricted use of lie detector tests, these claims may become more common in the future.

At least one major state court *rejected* an employee's tort claim for negligent administration of a polygraph exam in 1990. The New York Court of Appeals held that the employee, allegedly forced to resign after failing a lie detector test, could not sue the private detective agency that administered the test. Writing on behalf of a unanimous bench, Judge Titone said that while the suit brought by former United Parcel Service Manager David Hall was not preempted by the federal Employee Polygraph Protection Act, the Act nevertheless "greatly diminishes the strength of the arguments for recognizing a new tort remedy at the state level." The New York Court of Appeals reasoned that the federal law establishes sufficient safeguards against improper testing and remedies for those who allegedly are injured by violations of the federal law.

Q. 62.26 Has the federal Employee Polygraph Protection Act produced much litigation so far?

According to an April 1990 report by Assistant Administrator Charles Pugh of the Labor Department's Office of Policy, Planning and Review, the federal polygraph law has produced very little in the way of legal actions. As of February 1990, the Department of Labor had received only 126 complaints of possible violations of the Act. At that point, the Labor Department had brought only one lawsuit into court, which was subsequently settled for $3,000 in back pay. Additionally, a public interest law firm in New York City had filed suit on behalf of a job applicant who alleged that she was denied employment for refusing to take a lie detector test.

Possible reasons for so little legal activity in this area include employer compliance with the law, employees' ignorance of its existence or application to them, effective Department of Labor enforcement, or use of alternative honesty tests (see Questions 63 and 63.1).

Q. 63 Are other types of honesty tests recommended?

Some pencil-and-paper honesty tests are well respected. And although numerous states now forbid, or severely restrict, the use of polygraphs, few have enacted similar restraints on pencil-and-paper tests. However, to avoid invasion of privacy and defamation actions, be sure that the job for which the individual is applying warrants such a test, and keep the test results strictly confidential.

There are basically three types of honesty tests. They are often given instead of polygraph tests. They include:

(1) The "overt integrity test," which asks about an individual's attitudes towards theft and other illegal activities;

(2) The "personality test," which is intended to predict workplace behavior with respect to dependability, job performance, and drug use as well as honesty; and

(3) The combination test, which combines both types of questions in an attempt to measure honesty.

Q. 63.1 What are the pros and cons of honesty tests?

Generally, these tests come under attack because of the uncertainty of their reliability to accurately measure a person's propensity for honest behavior.

On the other hand, paper-and-pencil integrity tests generally are not prohibited by federal or state law, and they have not aroused the same vociferous animosity and distrust of labor unions, civil liberties groups, and so forth as polygraphs. Some well-established testing companies claim high correlations between test results and later employment experience. But it is important to track hiring patterns in relation to test results. If honesty testing leads, for example, to an above-average rejection rate for minority applicants, the test could be held to have an illegal adverse impact on that minority group under federal or state discrimination laws. A second caveat: pencil-and-paper tests may well be the next target of lawyers and organizations that oppose any such intrusion into employees' privacy. Some polygraph statutes (e.g., in Massachusetts) may already be broad enough to cover pencil-and-paper tests. Employers should keep abreast of new legal challenges in this area.

Q. 69 Can applicants and employees be tested for drugs?

A preemployment physical may include a urine or blood test, which can detect substance abuse. It may also be appropriate to request that an employee be tested if his or her behavior at work suggests the use of drugs or alcohol. Refusal can be characterized as insubordination, resulting in termination of employment. However, random testing of employees without any reason to suspect drug abuse has been ruled a constitutional violation by a number of courts with respect to public employees, and probably is a legally risky policy in the private sector as well.

At present, the status of drug testing in the workplace is uncertain. A federal judge recently granted an indefinite extension on a ban for drug testing of Detroit police officers. The opinion notes that in the absence of proof of a widespread problem among the police officers, it is inappropriate to subject the officers to drug tests.

In New Jersey, however, a municipal drug-testing plan that required police officers to submit urine samples during their annual physical examinations and that also permitted testing on a random basis was held not to violate the officers' Fourth Amendment rights. The Court of Appeals for the Third Circuit held that the administration search exception to the Fourth Amendment's protection against warrantless searches applied because police officers belonged to a pervasively regulated profession, which justifiably reduces their expectation of privacy on the job. (*Policeman's Benevolent Association Local 318 v. Township of Washington,* Dkt. No. 87-5793 (3d Cir. (1988))

In line with the Third Circuit's decision, the Pennsylvania appellate court has upheld Philadelphia's policy requiring police officers to be tested for drug use when there are grounds for reasonable suspicion and when the officers return from extended leaves or are reinstated, promoted, transferred, or reassigned to special units. In upholding the city's "Directive 55" drug-screening policy, the court concluded that such a policy was "inherently managerial" and therefore within the properly exercisable rights of the police commissioner. (*Copeland v. Philadelphia Police Dept.,* 840 F.2d 1139 (3d Cir. 1987)) (See also Questions 608.13–608.15.)

Q. 69.1 How is the Drug-Free Workplace Act of 1988 affecting employers?

On November 18, 1988, the Drug-Free Workplace Act became law as part of the omnibus antidrug legislation approved by Congress. Although the law is complicated, the Office of Management and Budget (OMB) recently issued guidelines to aid federal agencies in enforcing the statutory requirement that federal contractors and grant recipients maintain drug-free workplaces. Although the rules and considerations embodied in this Act are complex, OMB's guidelines, which are published in the *Federal Register,* provide a detailed question-and-answer section for implementing the Drug-Free Workplace Act. However, several courts have already been called upon to resolve challenges to the new Act. Because the status of the law is presently unclear, employers would be wise to adopt a wait-and-see approach to the law. (See Questions 608.1–608.15.)

Q. 108.1 How much privacy must an employee be permitted?

The answer to this question depends on many factors. First, an employee's privacy is dependent on whether the employer is a government agency or a private party. For instance, a professor at a state university may be entitled to constitutional protections that colleagues at a private liberal arts college are not. In other words, it has often been said that the Bills of Rights stops at the factory door (although some labor arbitrators have from time to time tried to invoke Fourth Amendment search-and-seizure rules and the like in deciding grievances).

Second, the collective bargaining agreement, if any, may limit management's right to invade employee privacy. Common law also sets limits on unreasonable invasions of privacy, and the standards vary from state to state. The bottom line is that an employer planning to investigate employee theft (or drug use) on its premises should proceed with great restraint. However, this does not mean that employers can do nothing. They have a right to protect their property, but in enforcing this right, employers must be ever mindful that they are brushing up against some cherished employee rights.

Q. 108.2 What procedures should an employer follow if it wants to conduct employee searches?

Employee searches may violate an employee's expectation of privacy. To prevent this from occurring, before implementing an employee search, employers should have reasonable cause.

It is suggested that employers:

- Defeat employees' expectations of privacy by notifying them that they can expect periodic searches.
- Conduct nondiscriminatory searches of all workers, including executives.
- Conduct searches using the least intrusive means possible.

- Have a union representative present during the search, if applicable.
- Suspend and arbitrate prior to discharging an employee who is found guilty of theft or substance abuse.

Q. 108.3 Can consent forms protect a company against liability?

Some employers require employees to give advance written consent to potential company searches of an office, desk, locker, or even the employee's car on company premises. Whether this exercise is effective depends on many factors. Public policy in most states does not permit an employee to waive his or her right to challenge future tortious activities by the employer. The employee may later argue that he or she did not sign the form voluntarily because employment (or continued employment) seemed to be at stake. An employee may argue that he or she did not knowingly sign the form because it was hidden in the fine print of a job application or other lengthy document. An employee may also claim that he or she did not anticipate the sort of search that ultimately ensued. Does all this mean employers should not use such consent forms if they plan to search employees for drugs or stolen goods? No. The forms may constitute a useful, maybe even a decisive, defense. But be aware that a consent form will not necessarily avert lawsuits.

Q. 108.4 How else can an employer lower employee expectations of privacy?

If an employer intends to conduct a search-and-seizure operation under certain circumstances, the policy should be promulgated at the earliest opportunity in the company's employee handbook and other appropriate media. This serves to lower the workforce's expectation of privacy and, thus, the chances of a successful lawsuit based on a tortious invasion of privacy.

Q. 108.5 Can a company electronically monitor employees?

The answer depends on *what* kind of monitoring is conducted, *why* it is being done, and *how* it is handled.

Concerning what kind of monitoring, many states have wiretap and eavesdrop laws that expressly forbid the secret monitoring of telephone conversations.

With respect to why the employer is monitoring employees, there should be a demonstrable business purpose. For example, personal computers might be monitored to check efficiency. Or telephones might be monitored to ensure proper sales techniques are being used.

Last, there is how the employer handles the monitoring. Advance notice to employees may circumvent a wiretap or eavesdrop statute by eliminating the element of secrecy. Notice may also diminish the employee's expectation of privacy, a necessary element in some states' common-law definition of the invasion of privacy tort, as well as in some Fourth Amendment search-and-seizure situations. Also, although employees may not like being monitored, a thoughtful employee communication program may help workers see the need, thus minimizing some of the predictable employee hostility and resentment. Hand in hand with this thought goes another: Monitoring should always be done with as much consideration as possible; for instance, telephone monitoring should not intrude on permissible personal phone calls.

Q. 108.6 Can a company photograph or film its employees on the job?

A common method of catching thieves in the act is to place a time-lapse video camera with a pinhole lens behind a wall or partition in the vicinity of the suspected employee's cash register, desk, or workbench. There appear to be no reported cases holding this sort of surveillance to be illegal in a private workplace. If the suspected activity occurs, the impact of this evidence can be devastating to the employee in any subsequent court action. However, patience is an essential virtue in surveillance situations, and a deep pocket is a prerequisite for the company that contracts out this work to a private detective agency. Time-lapse cameras can show time and date on the videotape. However, many security professionals feel strongly that an operator, who later can verify the authenticity of the pictures by his or her live testimony, be present at all times. Time-lapse cameras raise another problem—editing what may be anywhere from several to many hours of tape so that a judge or jury sees only the critical events or transactions. In short, videotape surveillance can be highly effective, but not in the hands of amateurs.

Q. 108.7 Are undercover agents an effective means of detecting employee crime?

When a company is convinced that a theft or drug ring is operating among its employees on the premises, "planting" a detective among the employees may be the most effective means of flushing out the culprits. Detective agencies usually charge an hourly rate for the planted employee; the rate is really a composite of the regular hourly rate received as one of the company's employees plus a premium to bring the total to the agency's regular rate. Agencies prefer to have the employer's help in establishing a cover story for the detective by setting aside an advertised job opening, accepting his or her application, and interviewing him or her as per the employer's usual practice. Then, as with time-lapse video surveillance, it becomes a waiting game, with the employee-detective being the employer's eyes and ears.

Q. 108.8 Should criminal charges be lodged against a dishonest employee?

An employer may want to file criminal charges for a number of reasons: to deter other employees, to involve the criminal justice system in the process of obtaining restitution, or perhaps to establish a record that clearly negates any chance of a defamation or wrongful termination suit by the discharged employee. Of course, the tactic can backfire if the ex-employee is ultimately acquitted. Sometimes, seeking a windfall and/or vindication, the acquitted employee may bring suit based on some sort of malicious prosecution theory.

Q. 108.9 Can a company threaten to bring criminal charges to gain some concession from a dishonest employee?

The threat of criminal prosecution lurks beneath many restitution agreements extracted from employees caught with their fingers in the till. From a legal standpoint, it is a misuse of the criminal justice process to use the threat of filing a criminal complaint to extract a confession, a release of claims, or a restitution agreement. Such a threat may itself be a criminal offense.

Coping With Labor Unions

Q. 117 Is labor unionism on the decline in the United States?

Union membership has steadily declined from a peak of 35% of the American workforce in the 1950s to less than 20% today. However, there has been growth in union affiliation among public employees (such as police and teachers), many of whom were not allowed to unionize until about 20 years ago. Unions seemed optimistic about resurgence in membership stemming from the growing dissatisfaction among white-collar workers (both clerical and professional) in the service and information sectors of our economy. Thus far, union success in these sectors has been mediocre.

In 1989 there was significant labor union activism, notably the grounding of Eastern Airlines in what was a strike of rare duration and intensity under the Railway Labor Act. Organized labor's advocates claimed that the Eastern stoppage proved that unions still have the muscle to shut down a major employer. Also, on issues such as minimum wage and right-to-know, the labor movement continued to play an important role. In southwest Virginia, the United Mine Workers of America (UMWA) conducted a militant strike against the Pittston Coal Company; spouses and children joined the protest with classroom walkouts and sit-ins of various sorts. Though shrunken in size, big labor will continue to be a significant presence, at least until the end of the century.

Q. 117.1 How well did organized labor perform on the organizing front during the past decade?

Organized labor did not fare well during the 1980s, according to an April 1990 article in Cornell University's *Industrial and Labor Relations Review* by Professors Gary N. Chaison and Deleep G. Dhavole. The professors report that since 1982 union certification elections in the private sector have yielded annual average net increases in union membership of only 43,000 employees per year. They comment that this number is "an almost inconsequential addition to the stock of 10.7 to 12 million union members in the private sector." They conclude that their study "confirms that the decline in union organizing is severe." They suggest that this decline "should give a new sense of urgency to ongoing debates over the barriers to union organizing, the effectiveness of the National Labor Relations Board (NLRB) in protecting employee free choice, and the future directions of a substantially smaller labor movement."

However, the unions' win-rate did improve somewhat in 1989. Unions reportedly won nearly half of their representation elections as the decade came to a close. According to NLRB statistics, the unions' win-rate was 45.9% in 1985, climbing to 48.6% in 1988 and 49.8% in 1989. The absolute number of representation elections also increased, with 3,506 in 1988 and 3,644 in 1989. These numbers can be misleading, however. The increased 1989 win-rate was shored up by a 71.8% rate of victory for *local, independent* unions in 195 elections. Unions successfully resisted only 31.2% of decertification efforts in 1989. These statistics hardly herald a major rebound by "Big Labor" in the 1990s.

Q. 117.2 Are there any union organizing tactics that seem to be particularly effective?

Various labor lawyers report that the so-called "corporate campaign" will remain an important union organizing tactic in the 1990s. A corporate campaign is generally a multi-faceted assault on the targeted company, including public relations efforts, government lobbying, and consumer boycotts. The relative ineffectiveness of stand-alone strike action has led to the development of this "shotgun" approach. However, targeted corporations may be on the verge of developing equally effective countermeasures, such as state law claims for tortious interference with business relations, trespass, and defamation.

Q. 126.1 Is an arbitration award enforceable when it contradicts a National Labor Relations Board decision?

An arbitration award that contradicts an earlier National Labor Relations Board (NLRB) ruling is unenforceable according to a case decided by the Ninth Circuit Court of Appeals. The union claimed that two related corporations under a double-breasting arrangement (whereby separate union and nonunion operations are run by a common owner) were alter egos, that is, the arrangement was created to avoid the employer's obligations under the National Labor Relations Act (NLRA). The NLRB agreed. Later, in the context of a grievance arbitration, the arbitrator ruled that the two firms did not meet the test of common or joint control. According to the federal court, the NLRB holding was binding. (*A. Darians & Sons, Inc. v. District Council of Painters No. 33*, No. 87-2799 (9th Cir., 3/8/89))

This case touches upon an issue that periodically haunts the grievance arbitration environment: How much attention must (or should) an arbitrator pay to public law when resolving a grievance and fashioning an award? Certainly an award that runs contrary to the law is unenforceable. But the arbitrator's charge is to fashion the award from the four corners of the labor contract. Sometimes public law and private law (the contract) are incompatible. Some arbitrators acknowledge a controlling public policy. Others adhere to the mandate of the contract and let a court overrule them on public law grounds in a later action to enforce or vacate the award.

Q. 126.2 When will the NLRB defer an unfair labor practice charge to arbitration?

When an employee files an unfair labor practice charge, but the employer demands an arbitration under the labor contract, the current NLRB practice is to defer the matter to the arbitrator *if* the unfair labor practice claim "implicates" a parallel provision in the collective bargaining agreement. However, some of the federal courts of appeals, which are charged with reviewing and enforcing labor board orders, have demonstrated their disagreement with this standard of deferral. For instance, during the past year, the U.S. Court of Appeals for the District of Columbia—probably the most influential of the 13 appellate courts on labor matters—stated that the NLRB should not defer unfair labor practice claims "that do not involve the interpretation application of collective bargaining agreements." In other words, just because some clause in the labor contract may be parallel to language in the Taft-Hartley Act, e.g., a clause forbidding discrimination by the employer based on employees' union affiliation—a common-enough clause, that clause does not free the board to defer its obligation to the private-party grievance procedure. How the NLRB will react to such criticism is unclear. Over its half century of existence, the NLRB has frequently held to its own course, unless (and until) the bulk of appellate court opinions stood against its view of the law or until overruled in its interpretation of the Act by the Supreme Court itself.

Q. 127.1 Can a union offer free medical tests to workers prior to a representation election?

The NLRB took the position in 1989 that free medical testing offered two days before an election so tainted the vote that the union victory had to be set aside. The union offered screenings for high blood pressure, lung functions, cholesterol level, and diabetes. The tests were given in two vans bearing the union logo. The NLRB concluded that workers who availed themselves of the tests believed they had gotten a gift from the union and that it was a benefit they would lose if they did not retain the union. This, the NLRB felt, was no different than an employer giving gifts during the campaign period. (*Mailing Services, Inc.*, 293 NLRB No. 58, (3/31/89))

Q. 135.1 What is the current status of the NLRB's rules on health care bargaining units?

In mid-1989 the American Hospital Association (AHA) filed a lawsuit challenging the NLRB's asserted power to mandate appropriate bargaining units by means of the administrative rule-making process. The 6,000-member trade association contended that Section 9(b) of the Taft-Hartley Act requires that bargaining units be determined on a case-by-case basis. (*American Hospital Assoc. v. NLRB*, No. 89-C-3279 (N.D. Ill., 1989)) A small irony in this lawsuit is that in the NLRB's more than half-century as an independent agency, the health care case is one of the few times the NLRB invoked its rule-making power. Historically, the NLRB has been content to develop its rules through case precedents.

In July 1989, the federal district court issued a permanent injunction, preventing the NLRB from enforcing its rules on health care bargaining units. The trial court held that these rules were inconsistent with the Congressional admonition against the "undue proliferation" of bargaining units within a single company, contained in legislative history dating back to a 1974 amendment of the National Labor Relations Act. However, this court order was not long-lived. In April 1990, the U.S. Court of Appeals for the Seventh Circuit, sitting in Chicago, vacated the lower court's order and gave the NLRB the authority to implement this historic rule-making. The AHA has vowed to seek Supreme Court review.

Q. 135.2 Are independent contractors covered by the National Labor Relations Act?

The easy answer is that independent contractors are not employees covered by the protection of the National Labor Relations Act (NLRA). The tougher answer is defining the difference between independent contractors and actual employees. As a general proposition, the definition depends on whether the company has the right to control how such workers perform their jobs.

Factors indicating that a person is an employee include working for only one employer, being provided work space, tools, and materials by the employer, and/or being required to be on the job at certain times on specified workdays. Factors suggesting an independent contractor status include allowing the worker to come and go as he or she pleases, allowing the worker to decide how to best accomplish the general goals set, and providing no fringe benefits to the worker by the employer. In a given situation, if most factors suggest an independent status, the worker has no NLRA protection with respect to labor organizing activities.

Last year, a group of rabbis, who performed "kosher kills" for a Chicago meatpacker were determined to be independent contractors, after they sought to be represented by Local 100-A of the United Food and Commercial Workers Union. The rabbis, known as "schoctim," were compensated on the number of kills they performed in accord with Orthodox Jewish principles, received no fringe benefits from the company, were not subject to the firm's disciplinary policy, and were accorded complete discretion on how they handled the slaughtering operation.

Q. 137.1 Is collective bargaining necessarily an adversarial exercise?

Typically in contract negotiations, both sides (or at least the union representatives) come to the bargaining table with a list of demands. The posture on both sides ranges from mildly to stridently adversarial, but this stance is not necessarily inevitable. For the past two years, the Labor Department's Bureau of Labor-Management Relations and Cooperative Programs has been working to develop a new collective bargaining model that seeks to emphasize mutual interests over confrontation. Deputy Under Secretary John R. Stepp, who heads the Bureau, announced in 1990 that research is close to completion. He cited the 1986 negotiations between General Motors and the United Auto Workers Union as a touchstone example in which the parties set forth common issues, rather than demands, for discussion. For the first time in the auto industry's history, a contract was consummated "without ever having to set a strike date," according to Stepp.

In an article entitled "To Confront or Cooperate? The Lesson of Anthracite Coal," in the *Labor Law Journal*, March 1990, James Castagnera suggested that "it cannot be proven that labor-management cooperation would have save the [coal] industry, but I believe this was the case. If I am correct, then Pennsylvania's anthracite coal industry stands as an articulate lesson to America's troubled smokestack industries, its old-line labor unions, and to all Americans." The bureau's new model is a step in the right direction for labor-management negotiations.

Q. 138.1 Is an employer's refusal to execute a collective bargaining agreement a continuing violation?

In 1989, the NLRB set aside an 11-year-old precedent when it ruled that it no longer intends to treat refusal to execute a labor contract as a continuing violation. From now on an employer's initial refusal to sign will start the clock ticking on a 6-month NLRA statute of limitations. In other words, the aggrieved union must file its unfair labor practice charge within that 6-month period or risk losing its opportunity for remedy thereafter.

Q. 138.2 Does the Taft-Hartley Act preempt a state law claim?

The common law recognizes a tort action for injurious interference with a contractual relationship. For example, a tort action has occasionally been invoked by one college or professional sports team against another for pirating away a coach. In 1989, a member of the Teamsters Union was able to sue the Seaboard Railroad System for allegedly getting him fired by his employer in retaliation for filing Occupational Safety and Health Act (OSHA) charges against Seaboard. Even though the union had grieved the discharge and an arbitrator had ruled against the employee, the employee was allowed by a federal court to proceed with his action against Seaboard, which was not a party to the Teamster labor contract under which the arbitration was brought. The terminated Teamster's tort theory was that Seaboard wrongfully interfered with his employment relationship.

By contrast, another federal court in 1990 refused to allow a coal miner to pursue a state law action against the United Mine Workers of America for alleged negligence in carrying out a mine inspection. The union's duty, said the court, came from the collective bargaining agreement. Consequently, the miner-member had to sue for breach of that agreement under Section 301 of the Taft-Hartley Act.

It is well settled, due to several Supreme Court decisions, that employment discrimination suits are not preempted by the grievance-arbitration procedures in labor contracts. Beyond that, however, at what point a disgruntled unionized employee can sue the employer and/or union outside the labor acts, the NLRB, and the collective bargaining agreement continues to be an evolutionary process on a case-by-case basis.

Q. 141.1 Can a state government require a nonunion contractor on a public works project to pay into a union apprenticeship fund and hire apprentices?

The federal Employee Retirement Income Security Act (ERISA) preempts a California administrative order that required public works contractors to support union apprenticeship programs. The programs are employee benefit plans, and therefore the bureaucratic order clearly fell into the "related to" category that triggers federal preemption. Also, the Taft-Hartley Act may trigger preemption, the federal judge who decided this issue held, because the state regulations required a nonsignatory employer to comply with the provisions of a union's collective bargaining agreement with other companies.

Q. 145.1 How far is a union entitled to go to protect employees' health and safety?

In 1989, NLRB ruled that Glass Workers Local 193 in Wilson, North Carolina, had the right to enter a glass container plant and take heat measurements. (*American National Can Co., Foster-Forbes Glass Division*, 293 NLRB No. 110 (4/28/89)) The NLRB derived its decision from a close analysis of the labor contract. One provision granted the union's international representative the right to visit plants to investigate grievances arising out of the interpretation or application of the contract. Another provision, entitled "Relief," called for "additional relief ... where heat or cold conditions warrant." Yet another clause required the company to "provide adequate heat, light, and ventilation to employees" and to "continue its best effort to devise systems to control drafts, noise, fumes, dust, grease, and job hazards." Putting all these provisions together, the NLRB concluded that the union had the right to collect the heat data.

Two observations, one practical and the other legal, may be appropriate here. First, heat levels constitute a very serious health concern in the glass making industry. Second, note that the NLRB looked to the collective bargaining agreement for guidance, not to the Occupational Safety and Health Act (OSHA) or elsewhere outside its own area of expertise.

Q. 145.2 What happens to a labor union when its leadership is guilty of racketeering?

During the past year, Roofers Union Local 30-30B was placed under a federal court "decreeship" in Philadelphia after 14 officers were found guilty of violating the Racketeer Influenced and Corrupt Organizations Act (RICO). (*U.S. v. Kane*, No. 86-451-15-16-17 (E.D. Pa., 7/17/89)) A court liaison officer was appointed by the federal judge to oversee the local's affairs: the union must adopt a grievance/arbitration procedure; all collective bargaining agreements must now be countersigned by the liaison officer; and the convicted former officers are barred from having any further contact with the union or any roofing job. The court took ultimate control of all union expenditures. It could have gone even further, by imposing a trusteeship and ousting the local's newly elected contingent of officers. Other unions that have been under Justice Department assault involving allegations of corruption include the Teamsters and Laborers. Time will tell whether the Bush Administration will actively pursue corruption within organized labor. The Philadelphia Roofers Union posed a particularly egregious example of such corrupt activity, because the U.S. attorney's net caught up judges who had accepted union favors and bribes.

Q. 145.3 Is an employee entitled to a jury trial in a Section 301 action?

In 1989 at least one federal court decided that the jury trial right adhered to a breach of labor contract case brought under Section 301 of the Taft-Hartley Act, which enables members to sue a union for breach of fair representation. But, strangely, the court also held that the employee had no jury trial right on the other side of the coin—his fair representation action against the union. Usually, breach of the collective bargaining agreement and breach of the duty of fair representation go together in a Section 301 suit by a union member claiming denial of his or her contract rights. Consequently, employers might reasonably expect both aspects of the suit to go to the jury, or both to be decided by the judge. But federal District Judge Mencer of Western Pennsylvania ruled that, although the breach of contract claim would have been recognized by eighteenth century common law—and thus must be accorded a Seventh Amendment jury trial—the duty of fair representation half of the suit is analogous to an unfair labor practice charge under the National Labor Relations Act (NLRA) and therefore cannot be decided by a jury. (*Nicely v. USX Corp.*, No. 88-0728, (W.D. Pa., 3/30/89))

The federal appeals courts are in disagreement about whether or not the Seventh Amendment jury trial right applies to fair representation cases. Recent decisions suggest a tilt against the right to a jury trial. But it remains for the U.S. Supreme Court to resolve the controversy when it is presented with the right case. Meanwhile there is speculation regarding whether juries will be more likely to favor labor unions or individual workers in such cases.

Q. 145.4 Can union members sue their union for leading them to commit illegal activities?

A group of former employees of Royal Harvest Foods, a poultry processing plant in Springfield, Massachusetts, is suing the United Food and Commercial Workers Union (UFCW) because a business agent induced them to conduct the wildcat strike that lost them their jobs. According to the evidence at trial, the business agent encouraged nonstrikers to join in once the wildcat was underway, saying that more participants were needed for the strike to succeed. The hapless members sued the UFCW for breach of its duty of fair representation under Taft-Hartley. The case is somewhat unique in the annals of fair representation cases, which more typically revolve around a union's poor handling of a member's grievance or some internal union discrimination tactic. For example, in December 1989, the Supreme Court held in *Breininger v. Sheet Metal Workers, Local 6* that discrimination in union hiring hall referrals gave rise to a "duty of fair representation" case. Overall, there seems to be a willingness within the federal court system to expand these causes of action by union members against their unions, when abusive practices occur. This willingness is perhaps one more sign of the declining influence of "Big Labor" in our national policy.

Q. 156.1 Can the hiring of replacement workers during a strike give rise to a good-faith doubt about the union's continuing majority support?

It is well established in labor law that a struck employer can hire replacement workers, assuming it can find new employees willing to cross the picket line. The company can even hire replacement workers on a permanent basis and not just for the duration of the strike.

Whether such permanent replacements can be considered pro- or anti-union has been a subject of substantial controversy for many years. The NLRB's view shifted back and forth over the decades, as the makeup of the board was altered by expiring terms and new Presidential appointments. As of 1990, the Board and the Supreme Court are in full accord that replacement workers will not be presumed to be either for or against the union. Consequently, because an employer has permanently replaced a majority of the striking workforce does *not* mean that the company can withdraw recognition from the union, claiming a good-faith doubt about the union's continued majority support.

Good-faith doubt has, in fact, become a very difficult position for a company to maintain. Good-faith doubt cannot be based on a "nose count" of replacement employees, nor can it be based on a secret-ballot private poll, since such a poll can itself only be justified by a good-faith doubt.

Q. 157.1 Is a company required to negotiate with a union over its decision to close the company?

The NLRB has held that a company is not required to bargain over management decisions that affect the basic nature or direction of the business. When labor costs are the basis for a decision to close, however, the employer is required to bargain over its decision to close. (*Otis Elevator Company (Otis II)*, 269 NLRB 891 (1984))

When an employer decides to close a plant entirely, as opposed to subcontracting or transferring work, the law permits the employer to make such a decision without bargaining with the union. Once the decision to close a plant is made, the employer is obligated to bargain with the union over the effects of the closure on bargaining unit employees affected by the closure. Employees' rights to job security, severance pay, pensions, and other accrued benefits are the types of issues that might be addressed in effects bargaining. As with any other negotiation with a union, an employer that has the duty to engage in effects bargaining is not required to grant any benefits or make any concessions. The only requirement is that the employer bargain in good faith. (NLRA, §8(d); see also, *J.D. Lunsford Plumbing, Heating and Air Conditioning et al.*, 254 NLRB 1360 (1981).) (See also Questions 696–711 regarding plant closings.)

Q. 163.1 Can labor unions picket employers' homes?

Last year the U.S. Supreme Court ruled that a Milwaukee municipalities law that banned picketing in front of a private home was constitutional. (*Frisby v. Schultz*, U.S. S. Ct., No. 87-168 (6/27/88)) The case arose from the picketing of a doctor's home by antiabortion activists. Although it was not a labor law case per se, the same principles seem to apply with respect to a union picketing an employer's home in the course of a labor dispute or organized drive.

Q. 166.1 Is the decision of the NLRB's general counsel to drop an unfair labor practice complaint, after the administrative law judge hearing has begun, reviewable?

The general counsel's withdrawal of a complaint after the hearing had started, but before any evidence on the merits had been introduced, was determined by the Ninth Circuit Court of Appeals to be an unreviewable, unappealable decision. This ruling expands the historically well-settled proposition that the general counsel's decision not to issue a complaint on an unfair labor practice charge is without appeal. (*Int'l Brotherhood of Boilermakers v. N.L.R.B.*, No. 87-7494, (9th Cir., 4/14/89))

Q. 166.2 Is it an unfair labor practice to fire unionized employees for drug use?

The NLRB general counsel has announced a policy of seeking reinstatement of employees who are fired after testing positive for drug use if the NLRB discovers that the employer failed to engage in good-faith bargaining with the employee's union before instituting the drug-testing policy. This pronouncement apears to be part of a coalescing policy position of the NLRB's counsel, the effect of which is that implementation of a drug-testing program without collective bargaining will in most cases constitute an unfair labor practice. The NLRB in Washington, D.C., recently heard oral arguments on this issue and will probably make a definitive pronouncement on it some time in the near future. Meanwhile, some labor specialists believe that a particularly strong management rights clause in a collective bargaining agreement may permit implementation of a drug-testing policy without prior union negotiation. However, at a bare minimum, employers must be aware that NLRB regional offices will closely scrutinize any unfair labor practice charges by unions that involve drug programs in the absence of negotiation.

Q. 169.1 Is the team approach to production legal under the National Labor Relations Act?

Last year, an NLRB administrative law judge ruled that a DuPont "design team" was actually an illegal labor union, created with the intent to undermine the union legally certified to represent team members. The design team included supervisors and dealt with issues that touched on mandatory subjects for collective bargaining. The Chemical Workers Association of the International Brotherhood of DuPont Workers challenged the arrangement. However, by the time that the administrative law judge pronounced the team to be an unfair labor practice, the design team had completed its objectives and had been dissolved, according to a DuPont spokesperson.

The DuPont design team experience raises the issue of whether other sorts of innovative team approaches might run amok of labor laws. Presumably collective bargaining of team concepts should solve the illegalities found in the DuPont case by the administrative law judge. A union may not always visualize at the bargaining table the sweeping changes in the labor-management relationship that a team concept can cause. A truly successful and effective team approach can undermine the traditional power of union business agents and stewards, short-circuiting the traditionally vivid lines of authority. Yet the team concept is highly conducive to the kind of labor-management cooperation many labor experts believe is essential for American industry to be competitive in a worldwide marketplace (see Question 137.1).

Employment Discrimination

Q. 173.1 Are there special hiring rules under Title VII with respect to American Indians?

Section 703(i) of Title VII of the 1964 Civil Rights Act has a special exception to the law's general nondiscrimination principles with respect to Native Americans. The law allows employers on or near an Indian reservation to exercise a preference for an individual because he or she is an Indian living on or near a reservation. During the past year, the Equal Employment Opportunity Commission (EEOC) clarified this provision, stating that it is applicable to areas containing large numbers of Indian tribes or a large Native American population where there are no reservations as such, for example, Oklahoma.

Q. 173.2 Are foreign companies doing business in the United States subject to the antidiscrimination provisions of Title VII?

Yes, a U.S. district court has recently held that foreign employers doing business in the United States must do so according to federal laws prohibiting discrimination. (*Ward v. W & H Voortman Ltd.*, 46 FEP Cases 1490, M.D. Ala. 1988)

Q. 173.3 Are American companies operating overseas subject to the anti-discrimination provisions of Title VII?

In February 1990, the U.S. Court of Appeals for the Fifth Circuit, sitting in New Orleans, by a 9-5 vote of the entire court, held that Title VII does *not* protect American citizens working for an American company in a foreign country. The court affirmed the earlier decision of a three-judge panel on the dismissal of the case of Ali Boureslan, a naturalized U.S. citizen, who had charged the Arabian American Oil Company (Aramco) with racial, religious, and national origin bias. (See *Boureslan v. Aramco*, 857 F.2d 1014, aff'd *en banc* 1990.)

This decision runs contrary to the position of the Equal Employment Opportunity Commission (EEOC), which has stated, ". . . if any American corporation operating overseas or a foreign corporation operating in the U.S. or overseas is 'engaged in an industry affecting commerce,' Congress intended there to be Title VII coverage. . . . The Commission therefore has the authority to accept and investigate these cases of employment discrimination. . . ." (*EEOC Compliance Manual* at 605:0057)

As with the National Labor Relations Board (see Question 126.2), the EEOC is free to adhere to its policy on Title VII's foreign jurisdiction, until Congress or the Supreme Court overrules the agency. Meanwhile some courts have agreed with the EEOC's position. (See, e.g., *Bryan v. Int'l Schools Services, Inc.*, 502 F. Supp. 472, D.N.J. 1980, *reversed on other grounds*, 675 F.2d 562.) In a worldwide marketplace, the American corporate presence abroad can be expected only to increase. The expansion will include enhanced activity in the East European nations, to name just one significant overseas opportunity. This international expansion emphasizes the urgency of Congressional or Supreme Court clarification on this Title VII issue.

Q. 177.1 What reporting and recordkeeping requirements are imposed by the EEOC?

Employers with 15 or more employees must annually file Standard Form 100 (Employer Information Report EEO-1, available from the Joint Reporting Committee, Federal Depot, 1201 E. 10 Street, Jeffersonville, IN 47130) and must retain a copy of the most recent report filed by each reporting unit at company or division headquarters. (Civil Rights Act of 1964, Pub. L. No. 88-352, §701(b); Equal Employment Opportunity Act of 1972, Pub. L. No. 92-261, §2(2)(b)) The EEOC has not adopted any generally applicable requirement that employers make or keep other employee records, although it has the authority to do so. It may also impose recordkeeping requirements on individual employers or groups of employers whenever it determines that such records are necessary for the operation of the EEO-1 reporting system or to further the purposes of Title VII.

To the extent an employer does generate employee records (including, for example, application forms and records of hiring, promotion, demotion, and so forth), it must retain the records for six months after the action or making of the record, whichever is later. An employer must keep a record of termination for six months from the date of termination. When a charge of discrimination has been filed, or an action brought by the EEOC or Attorney General under Title VII, the employer must retain all relevant personnel records until final disposition of the matter. (EEOC, 29 C.F.R. §§1602.7 and 1602.14 (1988))

Q. 189.1 Can an employer that has been found guilty of discrimination against an employee be made to pay prospective as well as back pay?

The usual remedy for a successful employment discrimination claim is reinstatement in the job previously held and back pay for the time lost on the job due to the employer's discriminatory act. However, it has been held that in unusual cases where reinstatement in the former job is not feasible because of "great antagonism between the employer and employee," an employee is entitled to "front pay," which is measured by the difference between what the employee is making in a new job and what the employee made in his or her former job, multiplied by the number of years the employee held the former job prior to being wrongfully dismissed. (*EEOC v. Red Baron Steak House*, No. C-86-552 (N.D. Cal., 6/2/88))

Q. 191 Has proving disparate impact recently become more difficult?

Yes. In a classic disparate impact case decided by the U.S. Supreme Court, a company had a rule stating that, except for the maintenance department, employees of all departments must have at least a high school diploma. (*Griggs v. Duke Power Co.*, 401 U.S. 424 (1971)) When the case was initiated, many more whites had high school diplomas than did blacks. Consequently, almost all of the positions outside the maintenance department were filled by whites, while positions in the maintenance department (the lowest department in terms of pay and status in the company) were filled almost exclusively by blacks. The Supreme Court declared that, although the requirement of a high school diploma was neutral on the surface, it had a discriminatory, disparate impact on black workers. Therefore, the policy violated Title VII.

However, since the appointment of Justice Scalia by former President Reagan, an increasingly conservative Supreme Court has made it more difficult for an employee to charge his or her employer with employment discrimination. In a decision announced on June 5, 1989, the Court modified its 18-year-old *Griggs v. Duke Power Co.* holding by increasing the burdens on an employee charging "disparate effects" discrimination. (*Wards Cove Packing Company v. Atonio*, 49 FEP Cases 1519, U.S.S.C. 1989). *Wards Cove* involved Alaskan salmon canneries at which unskilled jobs were filled predominately by nonwhites and skilled jobs were filled predominately by white workers. The employees based their claim of discriminatory hiring practices on this disparity. The Supreme Court, however, held that a mere showing of different racial proportions in various jobs was insufficient to support a claim by the workers. Instead, the workers had to show that the percentage of nonwhites in skilled jobs was out of balance with the percentage of nonwhites who *applied* and *were qualified* for the jobs. In this case, the Court held that the workers had not shown the requisite imbalance between the qualified worker pool and the hired skilled workforce.

Further, the workers were required to point to specific employment practices that had demonstrably caused the disparity; it was not enough to state that "overall practices" caused an imbalance. Finally, even if the workers had proved that specific employment practices had a discriminatory impact (still assuming no intention to discriminate), the employer could defend its actions by providing a reasonable business justification for them; it would be up to the workers to show that the company's explanation was inadequate.

Q. 191.1 What has been the impact of the Supreme Court's *Wards Cove* decision since it was announced in June 1989?

At least one U.S. appellate court has had the opportunity to apply *Wards Cove Packing Co. v. Atonio* (see Question 191) in a case of its own. In *Green v. USX Corp.*, 89G F.2d 801, the Third Circuit held that the evidence that the company's hiring practices for unskilled workers at a Pennsylvania plant discriminated against black applicants was good enough to establish liability, even under the Supreme Court's new, tougher disparate impact test. *Green* grew out of a 1976 class action against USX's predecessor, United States Steel Corporation, under Title VII on behalf of thousands of black job-seekers who unsuccessfully competed for production and maintenance jobs at the firm's Fairless Works. The court found that the plaintiffs had presented sufficient evidence to support a trial court's finding that the employment interview at Fairless had a disparate impact on black applicants. Consequently, concluded the court, the *Green* plaintiffs had met the *Wards Cove* test.

It is too soon to draw definite conclusions on where *Wards Cove* has left disparate impact as a legal alternative to proving intentional (disparate treatment) discrimination. But *Green* suggests that disparate impact (essentially guilt through unintended discrimination by a racially-neutral personnel policy or procedure) is alive and well in the federal courts.

Q. 191.2 When subjective or discretionary criteria are used in employment decisions, must an employee prove that the employer intended to discriminate in order to prevail in a Title VII action?

In the past, courts have applied separate standards to employment decisions that were based solely on objective criteria, such as standardized tests, and subjective criteria, such as personal judgment or the application of inherently subjective criteria. When only objective criteria were used, courts applied the so-called disparate impact analysis. If an employee could show, to a statistically significant degree, that such objective criteria disproportionately affected a protected class, and that such criteria were not related to job performance, a court would find an employer liable under Title VII—even if the employer had not intended to discriminate. However, for cases in which an employer used only subjective criteria, courts would apply a "disparate treatment" analysis under which an employee had to prove that an employer intended to discriminate. A showing of disproportionate impact alone would not be sufficient.

In a recent case, the Supreme Court held that in "mixed" cases, when both subjective and objective criteria are used, the process is correctly considered to be subjective, and the disproportionate impact analysis is appropriate. Consequently, an employee does not have to prove intent to discriminate to prevail. The ruling makes prevailing in mixed cases easier for employees because they no longer have to prove discriminatory intent. Consequently, employers' exposure to successful Title VII claims is increased. (*Watson v. Fort Worth Bank & Trust Co.*, 56 USLW 4922 (Jan. 20, 1988))

Q. 196.1 Can an employer be held accountable for racially motivated harassment in the workplace?

Under Title VII, a racial harassment action can be brought against an employer when the employee claims that the employer subjected the employee to a racially hostile work environment. To establish a cause of action under a racially hostile workplace theory, the employee must show (1) racially motivated conduct resulting in an unreasonably abusive or offensive work environment that makes the employee's job more difficult, and (2) that the employer tolerated or condoned the situation. Employers that take reasonable steps to correct and/or prevent racial harassment in the workplace will not be found to have violated Title VII. Consequently, employers should take quick and appropriate action to remedy the situation when they become aware of racially motivated conduct in the workplace that could conceivably constitute harassment.

Q. 204 What is reasonable accommodation of an employee's religious beliefs?

An employer may be required by law to allow an employee to wear a costume, headpiece, or emblem peculiar to a particular religion, or to allow the employee to work out a schedule that permits absence on religious holidays. However, the emphasis is on "reasonable." For instance, a company is not required to force some employees to work every Saturday so that a Seventh Day Adventist can observe the Saturday sabbath. Nor must an employer allow a Muslim to wear a turban in lieu of a hard hat if job safety requires the hard hat.

Firing an employee who refuses to work on his or her sabbath may leave an employer open to a charge of religious discrimination. Section 701(j) of Title VII requires that, absent undue hardship, an employer must reasonably accommodate the religious needs of its employees. Consequently, before an employer may fire such an employee, it must be sure that no reasonable accommodation of the employee's religious belief is possible without undue harm to the business. Increased costs to the employer, if significant, may constitute undue hardship.

Q. 205.1 Are employment decisions that are based on sexual stereotypes actionable under Title VII?

Yes. The Supreme Court has recently held that an employer's use of sexual stereotypes in deciding whether to make a female employee a partner in an accounting firm could lead to employer liability under Title VII. (*Price Waterhouse v. Hopkins*, 57 USLW 4469, May 1, 1989) Remarks or evaluations stating that a woman is "too macho," "too aggressive," "uses lewd language," or "lacks femininity" are all problematic for employers. If such remarks were made in the workplace or during an evaluation process, an employer should take steps to show that no reliance was placed on such remarks in arriving at any employment decision.

If it can be shown that both permissible and impermissible criteria were used (a "mixed motive case") in arriving at an employment decision, an employer is not liable under Title VII, if most of the evidence shows that the employer would have made the same decision if it had considered only the permissible factors. Clearly, an employer will not prevail in a mixed motive case if it justifies its employment decision with permissible criteria that were not actually used at the time of the original employment decision. In short, to win, an employer must show by the weight of the evidence that a legitimate reason, relied on during the original employment decision and standing alone, would have resulted in the same decision. Without such a showing, an employer will be found liable in a mixed motive case. In view of the above, employers should examine their employee evaluation practices to determine whether stereotyped views or notions are present, and if so, remove them.

Q. 205.2 Can an employer discharge an employee because of pregnancy?

No. Private employers with 15 or more employees are subject to the federal Pregnancy Discrimination Act (42 USCA §2000e-2), which prohibits discriminatory treatment of pregnant women. Consequently, employers may not discharge an employee because of pregnancy or treat pregnancy-related disabilities differently from any other temporary disability. Employers should develop a neutral disability and sick leave policy and make certain that the policy is administered so that it does not discriminate against pregnant women.

Some general guidelines an employer can follow are:

- A pregnant woman may not be denied any job solely because she is pregnant. (See Question 56 in the main volume.) Any decision made must be based on her ability or inability to work.
- A pregnant worker may not be required to take a leave of absence if she is able to perform her job duties.
- A pregnant worker who requests maternity leave is entitled to it on the same basis that leaves are granted for other temporary disabilities. (See Question 396 in the main volume.)

Q. 205.3 Can an employer require a pregnant woman to return to work within a specified period of time after delivery or after a physician has certified that the woman is capable of returning to work?

Generally, yes, as long as the employer can support such a policy by a business necessity. Courts have upheld policies that require women to return to work within 60 days of delivery or upon certification of capability by a physician.

Q. 205.4 Must an employer guarantee to reinstate a pregnant worker in the same position she held prior to maternity leave?

An employer is not required to return an employee to the position she occupied prior to maternity leave. However, if the employer guarantees reinstatement in the same job to persons who return to work from disability leave for nonoccupational illness or injuries, other than maternity leave, the practice would be considered discriminatory. Consequently, an employer that extends reinstatement to employees after periods of temporary disability must pursue the same policy when the temporary disability is caused by pregnancy.

Q. 205.5 When a woman returns to her job after a pregnancy leave, may her seniority or benefits be affected?

No. An employer may not reduce an employee's seniority or benefits due to a pregnancy-related leave of absence.

Q. 205.6 Can a company lay off a pregnant employee as part of a fetal protection program?

As with the applicability of Title VII to Americans working for U.S. companies abroad (see Question 173.3), the EEOC seems to be in conflict with one or more federal courts of appeals on the issue of fetal protection policies. In September 1989, the U.S. Court of Appeals for the Seventh Circuit (Chicago) approved a battery plant's rule that prohibited all pregnant employees from the premises. (See *United Auto Workers v. Johnson Controls*, 50 FEP Cases 1628.) However, the EEOC says such fetal protection policies "are facially discriminatory and cannot be easily justified." Consequently, a 1990 EEOC policy statement informed EEOC field offices not to rely on the Seventh Circuit's ruling as guidance in processing similar sex discrimination charges in states outside that court's jurisdiction (which is Illinois, Indiana and Wisconsin). Meanwhile, as this Supplement goes to press, the Supreme Court has agreed to review *Johnson Controls*, presumably to resolve the court-agency dispute over this issue.

Q. 207 How will a court determine the presence or absence of sexual harassment in the workplace?

Although at one time only the exchange of sexual favors for preferential treatment on the job was considered sexual harassment subject to sanction under Title VII, the current definition is much broader. Today, courts consider any unwelcome sexually oriented behavior—which need not result in physical contact—that creates a term or condition of employment to be sexual harassment. Sexually suggestive comments alone may constitute sexual harassment under Title VII if they create a work environment that the employee feels is hostile, abusive, or offensive. Sexual harassment need not involve the conditioning of concrete employment benefits on sexual favors. Specifically, a successful claimant does not have to prove a loss of any economic benefit, but only that, given the "totality of the circumstances," the employment environment is hostile, abusive, or offensive as a result of sexually suggestive conduct. (*Meritor Savings Bank, FSB v. Vinson*, 106 S. Ct. 2399 (1986))

Q. 208 Is the company responsible for sexual harassment of one employee by another?

In so-called hostile environment cases, when an employee alleges no loss of economic benefits resulting from sexual harassment, an employer will not be found automatically liable for any act of sexual harassment by a supervisor. However, courts will find an employer liable for a supervisor's sexual harassment of a subordinate if the employer had actual knowledge or, given the circumstances, should have had knowledge of the supervisor's actions. Also, an employer will be held strictly liable for a supervisor's discriminatory discharge of an employee if, under common-law principles of agency, the supervisor was acting within the scope of his or her actual or apparent authority.

When the harassment stems from a worker on the same organizational level as the person being harassed, the company may not be liable unless the victim complains to upper management. Once a complaint is made, the company must take prompt, effective action in order to avoid liability.

In one case, a district court in New York held an employer liable for sexual harassment by nonemployees. (*EEOC v. Sage Realty Corp.*, 507 F. Supp. 599 (S.D.N.Y. 1981) The employer required a female employee to wear a revealing uniform, which prompted customers to make sexually suggestive comments. When the employee refused to continue to wear the uniform, she was fired. The court held the company liable because it was aware of the sexual harassment and yet refused to take appropriate action to eliminate it.

Q. 208.1 To successfully bring a claim of sexual harassment, must the complainant be the actual subject of sexually suggestive behavior?

No. An employee who was never directly subjected to sexual harassment may nevertheless bring a successful claim for sexual harassment under Title VII. Although not themselves singled out for unwanted sexual attention, if employees can show that co-workers were the subject of such sexually oriented behavior, and that as a result those co-workers who complied were granted favored treatment, the employees can allege that the employer created a work environment that was hostile, abusive, and offensive. If the facts support such an allegation, the employer will be liable for sexual harassment under Title VII.

Q. 210.1 Should an employer discourage sexual contact outside the workplace between supervisory personnel and subordinate employees?

A policy that discourages such contact is advisable. An employee who has voluntarily engaged in sexual relations with his or her supervisor may later claim that such relations were unwanted and that he or she was afraid of being fired. Such an allegation constitutes a foundation for a claim of sexual harassment under Title VII, despite the fact that the conduct was voluntary. The Supreme Court has held that the fact that sexual relations were voluntary is not a defense to a Title VII suit for sexual harassment. (*Meritor Savings Bank, FSB v. Vinson et al.*, U.S. S. Ct. Dkt. No. 84-1979 (1986)) The key is whether, albeit voluntary, the relationship was "unwelcome." Supervisors should be especially sensitized to this potential problem regarding subordinate employees.

Q. 210.2 How has the law on sexual harassment developed during the past year?

During 1990, a number of federal courts across the country have rendered sexual harassment rulings that continue the shape the contours of the federal common law. In Pennsylvania, two female policy officers won the right to a new trial in their Title VII suit against the city of Philadelphia. According to an appeals panel, the trial judge had placed too much emphasis on lack of physical contact and sexual advances, when ruling against the two women. The appellate panel instructed the judge to refocus on allegations of a "hostile and intimidating work environment," including "alleged verbal obscenities, pornography in the workplace, destruction of personal property, and threatening, anonymous phone calls." The standard for liability seems to be whether or not such activities, if proven, would intimidate "women of reasonable sensibilities."

Also in 1990, another appellate panel held that a Puerto Rican bank violated Title VII when it fired an employee who became pregnant from an extramarital affair with her supervisor. The bank apparently had been aware of the affair for several years. Only when she was pregnant did her employer fire her and her supervisor, the bank's assistant controller. In its defense, the bank pointed to its rule requiring its employees to "maintain at all times conduct characterized by decency and public morality." However, the real reason for the dismissal was found to be her pregnancy, and that, in turn, was found to be an illegal discriminatory motive.

If getting pregnant by a supervisor isn't a proper ground for discharge, what about promoting a paramour? Well, somewhat surprisingly, the EEOC said in a policy guideline to its field people, that sexual favoritism to a spouse or friend "may be unfair," but is not necessarily illegal. Since both male and female workers sometimes suffer disadvantages and unfairness in the workplace "for reasons other than their genders," favoritism based upon a mutually-agreeable sexual relationship might not, in and of itself, violate Title VII. However, widespread favoritism of this type in a company could meet the "hostile work environment" test since a supervisor who coerces an employee to grant sexual favors for workplace advantage may give rise to actions by both the victim of the unwelcome advances and his/her co-workers, who were denied a fair opportunity to compete.

These developments suggest that the emphasis is shifting to "hostile work environment" as the focus of Title VII enforcement against sexual harassment. Willing sexual relationships between co-workers, even when they result in pregnancy or promotion, are not per se illegal activities nor do they clearly call for company discipline. However, unwelcome advances or demands, as well as inappropriate personal behavior that would offend "women of reasonable sensibilities," will give rise to Title VII violations.

Nonetheless, sexual relations between supervisors and subordinates should be discouraged (see Question 210.1). None of these new developments indicates such a rule is either improper or illegal.

Q. 212 What is handicap discrimination?

The definition of handicap discrimination varies somewhat from law to law, but generally covers employment decisions based on an employee's *non-job-related* disability. Handicap discrimination is not forbidden by Title VII of the 1964 Civil Rights Act, although many state human rights acts make handicap discrimination illegal.

At present, federal law forbids handicap discrimination only by government agencies and federal contractors. However, last year a comprehensive civil rights bill, prohibiting handicap discrimination by all private employers, was introduced into both houses of Congress, and will undoubtedly receive further consideration in future congressional sessions. More than 50 handicapped rights groups support this legislation. Meanwhile, many state antidiscrimination laws already forbid employment discrimination against the handicapped. (See H.R. 291; S. 933/H.R. 2273; and S. 47/H.R. 655 in Appendix B.)

Q. 212.1 How does the federal Rehabilitation Act of 1973 define a "handicapped individual"?

There are three elements of the Rehabilitation Act's (29 USC §706(7)(b)) definition of a handicapped individual: The person (1) has a physical or mental impairment that substantialy limits one or more major life activities, (2) has a record of such an impairment, or (3) is regarded as having such an impairment. (See also Question 246 in the main volume.)

Q. 212.2 How does the federal Rehabilitation Act define a "private employer"?

The federal Rehabilitation Act, which prohibits employment discrimination based on a handicap against persons otherwise qualified to perform a job, does not apply to private employers. However, all federal contractors and any federal financial assistance recipient is not considered to be a private employer and comes within the scope of the Act. Consequently, seemingly private employers, such as hospitals, that receive federal financial assistance are subject to the provisions of the Act. (See also Question 246 in the main volume.)

Q. 213.1 Can an employer refuse to hire a person with a non-job-related handicap?

In general, courts will uphold an employer's right to deny employment to persons with high blood pressure, epilepsy, or diabetes, as well as alcoholism or drug addiction, if the handicapped individual fails to take steps to correct or control the condition. As an example, New York City was able to sustain its decision not to hire a diabetic to drive a garbage truck in Manhattan. In the face of a legal challenge, the city proved a danger to public safety in permitting a person prone to blackouts to drive a truck that may at times weigh 30 tons. The driver not only admitted that his condition had become severe, but also acknowledged his failure to control his condition. (*Serrapica v. City of New York*, No. 88 CIV 2040, (S.D. N.Y., 3/14/89))

Of course, the other side of the coin is that courts often require employers, under a reasonable accommodation theory, to give the afflicted employee at least one opportunity to get corrective treatment before terminating employment on the basis that the handicap is job related.

Q. 213.2 Is high blood pressure a non-job-related handicap?

In an increasing number of states, high blood pressure is viewed as a handicap. If the condition can be controlled by medication, it probably cannot constitute a bona fide reason to deny employment to a hypertension sufferer. But if the worker refuses or neglects to control high blood pressure, an employer may be justified in suspending him or her, or at least transferring the employee from a dangerous job, until the problem is under control.

Q. 213.3 Is poor eyesight a non-job-related handicap?

Courts and agencies around the country seem to be divided on whether an employee with poor eyesight should be classified as a handicapped employee. One camp holds that simply needing to wear glasses does not make an employee a handicapped individual for purposes of discrimination protection. However, there is another camp forming that believes not only that eyeglass wearers should be treated as handicapped under the law if they are discriminated against in applying for jobs (such as by police departments), but also that indeed any such eyesight requirements should give way, even in police and fire departments, in light of modern technological advances in eyewear.

Q. 213.4 Is pathological gambling a non-job-related handicap?

In a lawsuit last year, an FBI agent who was fired for gambling with funds he was issued as part of an undercover assignment convinced a federal judge that his compulsive gambling was a handicap under the Rehabilitation Act. (*Anthony P. Rezza v. U.S. Dept. of Justice et al.*, Dkt. No. 87-6732 (E.D. Pa. 1988)) After the gambling incident, the agent had entered a 22-day treatment program, and thereafter attended Gamblers' Anonymous twice a week. The Rehabilitation Act specifically covers both "physical and mental impairment," and the implementing regulations cover psychological disorders, mental retardation, emotional and mental illnesses, and learning disabilities. The agent had to satisfy the court that he was actually impaired and that he was otherwise qualified to perform his job. Whether this case will serve as guiding precedent for state courts in determining an addicted gambler's rights under applicable state antidiscrimination laws may turn on how a specific state law and regulations are written. But, assuming that compulsive gambling is generally accepted as a genuine mental disorder, there is no obvious reason it should not be treated as a handicap, as is alcoholism.

Q. 213.5 What is the status of the Americans with Disabilities Act?

On July 26, 1990, President George Bush signed the Americans with Disabilities Act (ADA) and ushered in the most sweeping antidiscrimination law enacted since the monumental Civil Rights Act of 1964.

Q. 213.6 What is a disability under the ADA?

A disability under the Act is (1) "a physical or mental impairment that substantially limits one or more major life activities," (2) a history of such an impairment, or (3) being regarded as having such an impairment. That last definition is the most difficult, and for employers the most legally dangerous, of the three. It can actually "pull people under the ADA umbrella" who are not actually disabled. Some examples may be helpful.

Example. A worker with a history of back trouble applies for a job. As a result of his pre-employment physical examination, the company learns of his history of sprains and strains. The applicant is physically fine now and has not had a back problem for several years; yet he is not hired. He is not disabled in the eyes of the doctor; but, in the eyes of the law, he is a victim of disability discrimination. Legally, he is one of those estimated 43 million disabled Americans the Act is aiming to protect.

Example. A convenience food store manager hires a new clerk. On his first day on the job, the new employee tells the cashier he has tested positive as a carrier of the HIV virus. She tells the manager, who finds fault with how the new clerk stocked the shelves, and fires him at the end of the day. He, too, is not disabled in a strict medical sense. He may have received a false positive test; or if he is actually an HIV carrier, he still may never develop AIDS. He may even have been joking about the positive test. Whatever the actuality, he has been treated as if he has a disability. Under the ADA, he is a victim of disability discrimination.

There are lots of other situations that the ADA could cover, where the existence of an actual medical or physical disability is unclear. Extreme obesity, high blood pressure controlled by medication, dwarves and midgets, and persons with unusual birthmarks are all good examples of conditions that may not be considered disabilities in a medical sense, but that would be covered under the Act. If the best qualified applicant for an office receptionist position is extremely obese or has a large red birthmark on his or her forehead, failure to hire that applicant would constitute disability discrimination. The new law demands that the disabled person be able to do the job, allowing for reasonable accommodation, without posing an unreasonable danger to himself or herself or to others. The Act does not permit looking good to be a criterion for hiring.

Q. 213.7 What is meant by "reasonable accommodation" under the ADA?

Reasonable accommodation is another area of ambiguity, and therefore likely litigation. There is a wide spectrum of possible approaches to this concept. The Pennsylvania Human Relations Act and the implementing regulations thereof do not define "reasonable accommodation," opting to leave it to case-by-case development. The Act and the regulations say only that the employer need not alter standards of attendance or productivity on the job to accommodate a handicapped worker.

By contrast, the Delaware Handicapped Persons Employment Protection Act, for example, is far more specific, enumerating four areas of accommodation that usually will be *un*reasonable: (1) providing personal appliances, such as eyeglasses and hearing aids; (2) reassigning regular duties from the handicapped employee to other workers without giving the disabled worker compensating tasks; (3) increasing the skill, effort or responsibility of co-workers in order to lighten the handicapped worker's workload; and (4) spending more than 5% of the handicapped employee's annual salary to make a physical change to accommodate his or her needs.

The federal Act seems to be taking a middle ground between these two extremes. Reasonable accommodation likely will include job restructuring, part-time or modified work schedules (such as "flex time"), modification or acquisition of equipment or devices, adjustment or modification of examinations and training materials, and possibly even provision of readers or interpreters. At what point the costs of these accommodations becomes unreasonable is unclear under the Act, but no doubt it is a function of the size and financial wherewithal of the employer, as well as the nature of the accommodation.

Q. 213.8 Is there a silver lining to this cloud on the horizon called the ADA?

In what continues to be a tight labor market throughout much of the Northeast, the ADA aims to tap an apparent reservoir of underutilized workers. This approach may work, not only because the Act forces businesses to better assess handicapped applicants, but also the wide publicity the new law has been receiving will encourage handicapped people who have heretofore been reluctant, possibly due to past discrimination, to enter the workforce.

With or without a silver lining, the ADA must be addressed. Predecessor state laws notwithstanding, the ADA signals an era of greatly increased sensitivity to the needs and potential contributions of handicapped workers in the American economy.

Q. 217.1 How may an employer proceed if it wishes to use medical examinations to show that an employee is unfit for duty or has breached the employer's policy regarding intoxicants?

An employer that conducts medical examinations of employees must be extremely sensitive to avoid offending the employees' personal rights. An employer should have a clear policy regarding prohibited conduct, and the circumstances under which medical examinations will be given.

The examination should be justified by a valid business reason. Once this is established, the examination should be administered on a nondiscriminatory basis.

Before an employee is required to undergo an examination, he or she should be apprised of the reasons for the exam and given an opportunity to discuss them. If an employee agrees with the employer that a problem exists, a medical examination may not be necessary.

An employer should have the employee sign a consent form to avoid liability for charges of assault and battery and/or invasion of privacy. The employer should select a qualified physician who is licensed to perform any necessary tests. It is a wise policy to insure the physician, and/or require him or her to carry adequate insurance.

An employer must keep all results regarding the examination strictly confidential to avoid infringing unnecessarily on an employee's right to privacy. It is a good idea to allow an employee an opportunity to submit independent medical opinions for consideration before any decision is made. (See also Questions 608.1–608.15.)

Q. 220 Are persons with AIDS or AIDS-Related Complex or who are carriers of the HIV virus "handicapped" under the Vocational Rehabilitation Act of 1973?

Yes. The Supreme Court has ruled that those with contagious diseases are handicapped for purposes of the Rehabilitation Act. (*School Board of Nassau County et al. v. Arline*, 107 S. Ct. 1123 (1987)) In this case, the contagious disease was tuberculosis, but the Court's ruling can be applied to cases involving AIDS and other infectious diseases. The Supreme Court's decision has been applied to reinstate a teacher who had been dismissed because of AIDS, and to find as handicapped carriers of the HIV virus who are perceived as dangerous and are therefore discriminated against. Therefore, those who actually suffer from AIDS, as well as those who are HIV carriers with no symptoms but who are treated as being impaired, are all covered persons under the Act.

Also, the Justice Department ruled that Section 504 of the Rehabilitation Act covers all people with AIDS and that no justification exists to single out AIDS as a basis for discharge.

This new Justice Department opinion supersedes an opinion issued earlier that said that if an employer feared AIDS might be contagious it could lawfully discriminate against the affected individual.

The extension of protections under the Rehabilitation Act does not mean that federal employers or federally financed programs cannot in individual circumstances exclude an AIDS-infected individual from the workplace. If an individual poses a threat to the health and safety of others or is unable to perform his or her job or satisfy the requirements of the program, that individual can be excluded if there is no reasonable way to accommodate these health and safety performance conditions. (See also Questions 219, 221, 224, and 596–608 in the main volume.)

Q. 220.1 Are private employers free to discriminate against persons with AIDS or AIDS-Related Complex or carriers of the HIV virus?

An employer that is not within the scope of the federal Rehabilitation Act may not treat persons with AIDS or AIDS-Related Complex or carriers of the HIV virus differently from those free of the disease. Many state and local governments have passed laws that specifically prohibit discrimination against people with AIDS or AIDS-Related Complex or HIV-positive persons. Accordingly, employers should keep abreast of their respective state and local legislative enactments.

Q. 220.2 Do persons with AIDS or AIDS-Related Complex or who carry the HIV virus constitute a direct threat to the health or safety of other workers?

The Rehabilitation Act exempts from coverage those handicapped individuals who present a direct threat to the health or safety of others in the workplace. However, because those with AIDS or AIDS-Related Complex and carriers of the HIV virus are considered in most cases to present no direct threat to the health or safety of others, they are not exempt and must be treated like everyone else.

Q. 221.1 How is the AIDS epidemic affecting the workplace?

Virtually all major firms in the United States report AIDS cases among their employees or employee dependents, according to a survey conducted by a New York City benefits consulting company. Apparently, AIDS is most prevalent in the transportation and communication industries, with 82% of the employers in each industry reporting cases of the disease. The lowest reported incidence was in the health services industry (30%) and the consumer product industries (47%). With respect to regional percentages, it appears that the AIDS epidemic is most prevalent in the Mid-Atlantic and the Pacific regions.

Most employers believe that their existing health plans are adequate to meet the increased demand of the AIDS epidemic. Ninety-two percent indicated no intention to modify their health plans. Among those firms that do plan such a change, 16% will institute pre-employment screening and almost 60% report that they will devise and implement an education program for their employees.

Q. 221.2 What should an employer do if it discovers that an employee has AIDS or AIDS-Related Complex or is an HIV carrier?

The employer and its agents must not allow the information to be circulated to other employees. To allow such dissemination may result in a public disclosure of private facts action against the employer, which may result in punitive as well as actual damages. Keep such information strictly confidential.

Some problem cases involving AIDS are resolved by allowing the employee to work at home or transfer to a different department. However, although these measures may be offered to an employee, they may not be forced on him or her.

The key problem in dealing with AIDS in the workplace is lack of understanding. Mediation, rather than litigation, is the preferred method for resolving disputes involving the disease. Generally, an AIDS education presentation should be incorporated into the regular training program. Bringing in someone to talk about only AIDS in a small company of 30 employees may engender fear of "who" or "if" anyone has AIDS.

Q. 221.3 How should a company go about developing an AIDS policy?

An employer could create a committee of upper management, supervisors, and employees that meets and discusses their concerns regarding AIDS and potential methods of resolving the issues. It is important for upper management to participate to send the right kind of message to employees. The committee should draft a proposal and issue a final plan companywide. The proposal should identify persons within the company who "need to know" if or when an employee has contracted AIDS. Assurances of the strictest confidentiality should be guaranteed.

An employer should deal with AIDS by developing:

(1) A well-advertised, well-understood policy;

(2) A core advisory team with key personnel who will become knowledgeable on the issues;

(3) A benefits protocol involving insurance, disability, and Social Security benefits and rights;

(4) A communications strategy on how management should respond when an employee identifies himself or herself as HIV positive;

(5) An educational program that includes a medical overview on AIDS and information on employee-employer rights and responsibilities; and

(6) A resource and referral service to let employees know what resources are available to them.

Q. 221.4 What level of monetary damages are the courts awarding in AIDS discrimination cases?

The April 1998 *Health Care Management Briefings* ran the following story:

". . . Hyatt Services has been ordered to pay $157,000 in an AIDS discrimination case. The firm was found guilty of removing one of its employees from his job because he had acquired AIDS. The award included $50,000 in punitive damages and reportedly is the largest judgment yet in an AIDS-related employment discrimination case. The court decision was the first under Pennsylvania's Human Resources Act which requires employers not only to accommodate individuals infected with HIV virus, but [also] to allow them to work at their accustomed jobs so long as they are capable of doing so. . . . Whether or not future plaintiffs will be able to collect [punitive damages] may depend upon a case now before the U.S. Supreme Court. In a case involving Pacific Mutual Life Insurance Company, the Court is expected to rule on whether huge punitive awards violate the "excessive fine" prohibition of the Eighth Amendment's guarantee of due process. In a separate AIDS-related case, an out-of-court settlement has been reached between a New York City hospital and a physician who contracted AIDS from a discarded needle. A $175,000,000 lawsuit had been filed by Dr. Virginia Prego against New York City Health and Hospitals Corporation which operates King County Hospital where Dr. Prego worked. The case was one of the first involving a health care worker who acquired AIDS on the job."

Q. 230.1 Is it age discrimination to place a deadline on an older employee's consideration of an early retirement package?

Last year, a federal court ruled that an early retirement offer to a group of nonessential salaried employees, which gave the employees only 15 days to consider it, did not amount to a constructive discharge—even though beneath the offer lay an implicit threat that their jobs might be eliminated at a future date. (*Bodnar v. Synpol*, 843 F.2d 190 (5th Cir. 1988))

Q. 233.1 Can an employee sue for age discrimination under ADEA even if he or she refuses to arbitrate the dispute?

Two years ago the U.S. District Court for the state of New Jersey has held that, even though an employee had an arbitration clause in his employment contract, he could ignore the clause and sue under the federal Age Discrimination in Employment Act (ADEA). (*Nicholson v. CPI International*, 46 Fair Empl. Prc. Case (BNA) (D. N.J. 1988)) This decision seems to be a logical extension of the U.S. Supreme Court's ruling a few years ago that a unionized worker is entitled to pursue a Title VII discrimination claim, whether or not the underlying grievance is subject to arbitration. (*Emporium Capwell v. Western Addition Community Organization*, 420 U.S. 50 (1975))

But in 1990, the U.S. Court of Appeals for the Fourth Circuit, sitting in Richmond, opened a split among the federal courts by concluding differently. Resolving what it perceived as a battle between the ADEA and the Federal Arbitration Act, this court held that an employee, who has agreed in his employment contract to arbitrate all disputes, must do so. He or she cannot sue in federal court at his or her sole discretion. (See *Gilmer v. Interstate*, No. 88-1796, 2/6/90.) Meanwhile, the U.S. Court of Appeals in Philadelphia affirmed the federal court in New Jersey on its *Nicholson* decision, so that it is now up to the Supreme Court (if it sees fit) to resolve this split among the appellate courts. Should the highest court ultimately concur with the Fourth Circuit's *Gilmer* approach, this decision could be a real benefit to employers who are willing to trade the opportunity to arbitrate for a shield against the possibility of more expensive and time-consuming litigation in federal court.

Q. 233.2 Are damages a plaintiff receives in an age discrimination claim subject to income taxation?

In 1989 the U.S. Tax Court held that damages awarded in a suit filed under the ADEA are subject to income taxation. The court agreed with IRS that compensation for lost fringe benefits is taxable income, even though the underlying fringe benefits would not have been included in gross income. The court hinted that liquidated, or double, damages (allowed under ADEA for willful violations) might not be taxable, but it was not considering this question. (*Wirtz v. Commissioner of I.R.S.*, TC Memo No. 1989-139, 3/30/89)

However, in 1990, the U.S. Court of Appeals reversed the Tax Court and held that neither back pay for lost wages nor liquidated damages is taxable. The court found that ADEA actions are, by nature, personal injury claims and, therefore, plaintiff's winnings cannot be taxed as income.

Q. 233.3 Can severance pay and supplemental unemployment benefits be reduced by pension benefits?

The EEOC's position, vindicated in a court case in 1989, is that laid off employees who are eligible for pensions cannot be denied the same severance and supplemental benefits given to their ineligible, usually younger, co-workers. For a company to offset one against the other, says the EEOC, is age discrimination. Even though the Employee Retirement Income Security Act (ERISA) under some circumstances permits pension offsets, ERISA's permission does not overcome the discriminatory impact of denying severance pay to pension-eligible employees in violation of the ADEA. (*EEOC v. USX Corp.*, No. 87-6044, (E.D. Pa., 3/22/89))

Q. 239 Does comparable worth continue to be a viable theory of sex discrimination?

Comparable worth seems to have lost some of its former luster as a theory of sex discrimination. This loss of popularity is partly because a number of courts have rejected the theory—usually following long and expensive lawsuits. But there have also been a few victories for the concept, especially in cases involving government employers. It is a difficult chore for plaintiffs to try to compare "apples and oranges"—e.g., to demonstrate that (predominantly female) secretarial jobs and (predominantly male) janitorial or maintenance positions deserve the same wages. And, even if successful, the court may require the litigants to show that the employer purposely structured the pay scales with sex in mind, or that women were discouraged from competing for the higher paying decisions. Little wonder that women workers continue to find the tried-and-true Equal Pay Act—which calls for equal pay between the sexes for substantially the same work—a more viable route to recovery of damages. For example, in a successful suit against a hospital during the past year, the court found that it was illegal to pay female custodians (classified as "aides") $0.11 an hour less than male custodians in the housekeeping department.

Q. 250.1 What is the process for bringing a claim of discrimination under IRCA?

A complaint must be filed with the Office of Special Counsel for Immigration-Related Unfair Employment Practices within 180 days of the alleged discriminatory act. The Special Counsel is directed to investigate each charge within 120 days of its filing to determine whether there is reasonable cause to believe the charge is true. If the Special Counsel finds reasonable cause, a hearing before an administrative law judge will be scheduled. If, as a result of the hearing, an employer is found in violation of IRCA's antidiscrimination provisions, sanctions will be imposed.

Q. 250.2 Who can file complaints alleging that they were discriminated against on the basis of their national origin or citizenship status?

Assuming a person is legally entitled to employment in the United States, the Office of Special Counsel for Immigration-Related Unfair Employment Practices will accept complaints only from a person who is a citizen or an alien who evidences intention to become a U.S. citizen. (See Questions 256–282 in the main volume and Questions 259.1–282.6 in this Supplement.)

Q. 250.3 Can an employer of 15 or more employees be subject to duplicate actions regarding discrimination before the EEOC and Special Counsel for Immigration-Related Unfair Employment Practices?

The Immigration Reform and Control Act (IRCA) specifically states that charges of discrimination cannot be filed with both the EEOC and the Special Counsel. An employee must choose one forum or the other.

Q. 250.4 Can employers mandate "English only" in the workplace?

The debate about "English only" in the workplace continues within the broader environment of conflict over what will be the official language of some of our states. The enormous Spanish-speaking populations of Florida, Texas, and California (three of our most populous states) have been agitating for wider recognition of their native tongue as standing at least on an equal footing with English. Predictably, this has evoked a reaction from some members of the English-speaking population, such as the U.S. ENGLISH Foundation, which supports California Proposition 63, an initiative that would declare English to be the state's official language. (The dispute reminds one of the long, ultimately successful struggle of

French Canadians to change the official language of Quebec.) Meanwhile, the courts continue to adhere to the rule that an English-only workplace rule must be supported by business necessity. Recently, a deputy clerk challenged the Los Angeles Municipal Court's English-only rule. In fact, in many U.S. jurisdictions the preprinted portions of pleadings (such as the notice on the face of the complaint concerning the time allowed to answer) are printed in both English and Spanish. And in the case cited earlier (*Municipal Ct. of S.E. Judicial District v. Gutierrez*, 109 S. Ct. 1736 104 L.Ed.2d 174 (1989)) enforcement of the rule was enjoined.

Q. 252.1 May an employer give preference to a citizen over an equally qualified alien?

Yes, a provision of IRCA states that it will not be considered an unfair immigration-related employment practice if an employer prefers a citizen over an equally qualified alien. However, if an alien entitled to employment in the United States is better qualified than a particular citizen, giving preference to the citizen may constitute impermissible discrimination.

The Immigration Reform and Control Act of 1986

Q. 260.1 Must an employer fire undocumented employees hired prior to the effective date of the Immigration Reform and Control Act of 1986 (IRCA)?

No. IRCA "grandfathers" workers hired prior to November 6, 1986. However, although the employer will not be subject to sanctions, the grandfather provisions of IRCA do not make it lawful for the unauthorized alien to accept employment. Consequently, the alien is still subject to deportation for accepting employment.

Q. 260.2 Is an employer allowed to fire undocumented workers hired prior to the effective date of IRCA?

A Chicago area hospital recently had to pay civil damages and a fine because it fired an illegal alien who had lied on his employment application. After Congress passed IRCA in 1987, the employee, Mr. Rodriguez, pursued the amnesty provision available under the Act. When he asked the hospital to provide him with a letter confirming his employment, he was terminated for having falsified his job application.

The Mexican-American Legal Defense and Education Fund instituted a suit on Mr. Rodriguez's behalf, maintaining that his termination was illegal and seeking civil damages. The Justice Department's

Office of Special Counsel also participated in this suit to enforce IRCA's antidiscrimination provisions. In announcing the settlement, Mr. Siskind of the Department of Justice stated that the hospital had "discriminated against Rodriguez by treating him differently from citizens that have falsified their employment applications but who had not been fired."

Q. 264 Are all employers covered by the antidiscrimination provisions of IRCA?

No, employers with 3 or fewer employees are exempt from IRCA's antidiscrimination provisions. Those employers with more than 3 but fewer than 15 employees are covered exclusively by the antidiscrimination provisions of IRCA. Employers with 15 or more employees are prohibited from discriminating on the basis of national origin and citizenship status by Title VII of the 1964 Civil Rights Act and are subject to the new provisions of IRCA only with respect to citizenship status claims filed with the Special Counsel's office.

Q. 267 What records must be kept for verification?

The employer and employee must fill out an Immigration and Naturalization Service (INS) form called an I-9. The I-9 form must be kept for (1) three years after the person is hired or (2) one year after the person is terminated, whichever is later. The I-9 contains a document checklist showing the evidence used to verify the employee's legal right to work. The I-9 form does not require that copies of the documentation be retained, but the employer may make copies and keep them on record. However, if copies of the inspected documents are retained, it may be possible for the INS to second guess the good faith of the employer in accepting such documents if they are later found to be forgeries.

The employer must also sign a sworn statement, under penalty of perjury, that, to its knowledge, the worker's documents are genuine.

Because IRCA limits the uses to which the I-9 forms and backup documents can be used, employers may have to keep such information in a file separate from employee personnel files to avoid any claim of their improper use by law enforcement agencies or the employer.

Q. 270.1 Must employment agencies and other persons or entities recruiting for a fee verify a prospect's employment eligibility?

Yes. Prior to recruiting for a fee or referring for employment for a fee, the entity must complete an I-9 form, even though the entity is not an employer per se.

Q. 274.1 Are other groups protected by antidiscrimination legislation?

Yes, under the terms of IRCA, U.S. naturalized citizens, permanent resident aliens, refugees, individuals who have been granted asylum, and newly legalized aliens are covered.

Q. 275.1 Can an employer use day labor to avoid the need to comply with IRCA?

Although employers are presumed to be in compliance with IRCA's verification procedures for the first 24 hours after an employee has been hired in order to give the employee time to produce the required documents, IRCA specifically forbids employers from using day labor to avoid compliance.

Q. 282.1 What do the antidiscrimination provisions of IRCA do that Title VII of the Civil Rights Act of 1964 has not already done?

The antidiscrimination provisions of the Immigration Reform and Control Act (IRCA) supplement those of Title VII in three important ways:

(1) They extend civil rights protections to aliens, a group not covered by Title VII.

(2) They expand the number of employers covered by antidiscrimination provisions from those with 15 or more employees (Title VII) to employers with 3 or more workers.

(3) They create an Office of Special Counsel and provide an alternative to EEOC determination of the presence or absence of discrimination in the workplace.

Q. 282.2 What conduct is prohibited by the antidiscrimination provisions of IRCA?

IRCA prohibits discrimination on the basis of an individual's national origin or citizenship status with respect to hiring, recruitment, or referral for employment. However, the antidiscrimination provisions do not apply when an employer's workers must be U.S. citizens for the employer to comply with federal or state law or regulations.

Q. 282.3 As currently interpreted, are employers liable for unintentional acts of discrimination against illegal aliens under the antidiscrimination provisions of IRCA?

The Special Counsel charged with enforcement of IRCA's antidiscrimination provisions has said that employers would be liable only if they intended to discriminate on the basis of a person's national origin or alienage. Employers are not liable for unintentional acts that nevertheless have a harmful impact on aliens.

Q. 282.4 What are the possible sanctions for violation of the antidiscrimination provisions of IRCA?

An employer can be ordered to pay back pay for up to two years and to pay civil fines of up to $1,000 for each individual discriminated against the first time, and up to $3,000 for each individual discriminated against for subsequent violations. In addition, if the employer is found to have been "unreasonable in law and in fact," attorneys' fees may be awarded to successful claimants.

Q. 282.5 Can illegal aliens sue employers for violations of the Fair Labor Standards Act?

At least one U.S. appellate court has held that, even though an illegal alien may be working in the United States in violation of IRCA, he or she is still entitled to sue a company that improperly pays minimum wages or overtime under the Fair Labor Standards Act (FLSA). The rationale behind this ruling is that IRCA and the FLSA have essentially the same purpose: preventing exploitation of workers.

Q. 282.6 Given passage of IRCA, are undocumented aliens protected by the minimum wage and overtime provisions of FLSA?

Yes. In spite of IRCA's passage, the Eleventh Circuit has held that an undocumented alien worker can recover lost wages under the minimum wage and overtime provisions of the FLSA. The court reasoned that bringing undocumented aliens within the scope of the FLSA would reduce the incentive to hire such workers at wage rates less than that demanded by law for documented aliens. (*Patel v. Quality Inn South*, No. 87-7411 (11th Cir., 6/8/88))

Q. 282.7 Is IRCA working as Congress intended when it passed this legislation?

According to a study released in 1990 by a New York State task force on immigration, employers in New York City are engaged in a "widespread pattern of discrimination against foreign-looking and foreign-born applicants as a consequence of the sanctions imposed on employers by IRCA." This conclusion was echoed in a subsequent report by the General Accounting Office. GAO's report found "widespread discrimination" against people who looked or sounded foreign-born.

According to Senator Edward Kennedy (D-Mass.), chairman of the Senate's Immigration Subcommittee, it is unlikely that either the Senate or the House of Representatives is ready to repeal IRCA's sanctions. Senator Kennedy was also critical of INS Commissioner

Gene McNavy, who proposed an extended outreach program to make companies and employers more aware of their respective rights and obligations under IRCA.

INS is revising its employer handbook in the face of a further GAO finding that companies are even less aware of IRCA's requirements than they were a year ago.

Employee Compensation

Q 288 What are minimum wages?

Minimum wages are the minimum hourly rates set by federal wage and hour laws. In 1938, when the Fair Labor Standards Act (FLSA) was passed, the minimum wage was set at 25¢ per hour over the course of the next seven years.

After vetoing Congress' first attempt in nine years to raise the minimum wage, President Bush signed a second, compromise minimum wage act in November 1989. As of April 1, 1990, the federal minimum wage moved up to $3.80 per hour. On April 1, 1991, the minimum hourly wage will be $4.25. However, the law also allows for a sub-minimum training wage of $3.35 per hour, going up to $3.61 on April 1, 1991. (See Question 320.4.) Only 25% of an employer's workforce can be paid the training wage at any one time and only until this part of the law expires in 1993. Violators are subject to the Fair Labor Standards Act (FLSA) back pay and liquidated damages provisions, and a $1,000-per-day penalty for repeated or willful violations can now be imposed in a civil action as well.

Q. 315.1 Has the term "willful," as used in FLSA, changed recently?

During the past year, the U.S. Supreme Court has adopted the definition of a willful violation of FLSA most employers favor. (*McLaughlin v. Richland Shoe Co.*, 486 U.S. 128 (1988)) An employer is guilty of a willful violation—triggering double damage liability—only when it acts with actual knowledge or reckless disregard of whether its compensation scheme violates FLSA. The Supreme Court rejected the Labor Department's suggestion that willfulness is present when the employer knows that FLSA may apply but proceeds without a reasonable basis for believing the procedures are in compliance with the law. Not only does a finding of willfulness lead to doubling of the back-pay award in some cases, but it can also trigger a three-year, instead of a two-year, liability period. The six justices who made up the majority felt that these sanctions were punitive in nature and therefore should be triggered only when a company has a fairly high level of culpability.

Q. 320.1 What are the recent trends in employee compensation?

A recent study by the Bureau of National Affairs (BNA) reported that financially troubled companies are implementing employee stock ownership plans (ESOPs) more often. Automatic pay increases seem to have given way to merit pay procedures. Many companies are introducing gain-sharing plans to encourage managers and the rank and file to cooperate and work together to improve productivity. Two-tier pay plans, once very much in vogue (especially in tandem with concessionary collective bargaining) seem to be losing their luster. On the other hand, lump-sum bonuses in lieu of pay increases—which unions at one point seemed to strongly resist—now seem to be catching on, turning up in about one-third of all union contracts.

Q. 320.2 Has there been a shift in companies' employment practices with respect to full-time vs. part-time employees?

Some studies conducted during the past year indicate that more and more employers are turning to part timers and temporary employees to supplement their regular workforces. Employee compensation and benefits strongly influence this decision. Often, employers can get away with paying part timers and temporaries lower wages or, if this is not possible, at a minimum they can avoid providing these employees with the same measure of benefits as their full-time co-workers. To some extent, these savings have been eliminated by Internal Revenue Code Section 89, which now requires that many part-time employees receive at least a pro rata share of the benefits employers give to full timers. (See Questions 321.16–321.17.)

Q. 320.3 How do U.S. wage rates stack up against other countries?

According to the Bureau of Labor Statistics, America still led much of the world in average manufacturing wages in 1989. The gap between American and European and Asian wage rates is not all that large. In some instances, foreign wages now surpass those in the U.S.

Compensation costs in Germany, Norway, and Sweden run 20 to 30 percent above the U.S. average. In Belgium, Denmark, Finland, Holland, and Switzerland, compensation costs are 5 to 15 percent higher than the U.S. average. Austrian, French and Italian wage rates are 90 to 95 percent of the U.S. average, while the Japanese rate is at 89 percent for the last full year with available figures.

Bringing up the rear, among America's toughest competitors, are Asia's new manufacturing "tigers"—Hong Kong, Korea, Singapore, and Taiwan—at a wage rate of only 23 percent of the U.S. average. All the same, their typical $3.32 hourly wage is substantially higher than the $1.16 (12 percent of the U.S. level) wage paid back in 1980.

Q. 320.4 Can an employer ever pay sub-minimum wages?

Under the Labor Department's interim rules on sub-minimum training wages, a company can (under appropriate circumstances) pay an employee, who is under 20 years of age, for up to 90 days of on-the-job training. This rule is in accord with the 1989 amendments to the Fair Labor Standards Act. There are, however, a number of regulatory requirements. For instance, the "total period that an employee may be employed at the training wage by any combination of employers may not exceed a cumulative total of 180 days." Therefore, an employer should know a trainee's employment history prior to paying sub-minimum training wages.

Q. 320.5 Are there any "hot" issues that have the Department of Labor on a "regulatory crusade" at present?

Child labor violations became a high-profile issue in 1990. In some respects, this seems almost anachronistic, conjuring up visions of "breaker boys" in the coal fields of 19th century Pennsylvania or Kentucky; but, in fact, the proliferation of fast-food restaurants and convenience stores has created a demand for teenaged employees. When the labor pool is small, companies may be tempted to employ teenagers too many hours and to ignore their operation of dangerous equipment, such as meat slicers. Responding to a perception of widespread abuses, the Department of Labor investigated some national fast-food restaurants, notably Burger King, during the past year, citing them for serious violations of the child labor laws.

On a completely different industrial front, a one-day "blitz" of 1,890 child labor investigations was conducted across the country in the garment trade and migrant labor camps, according to congressional testimony by Assistant Secretary (for employment standards) William C. Brooks.

The clear message to employers is not to take these hoary old child labor laws for granted.

Employee Fringe Benefits

Q. 321.1 What is the current status of Section 89 of the Internal Revenue Code of 1986?

With uncharacteristic swiftness, Congress and President Bush have approved H.R.J. Reg. 280, which contains a provision that repeals the controversial Section 89 of the Internal Revenue Code of 1986. The repeal, attached to a measure increasing the limit on government debt, was passed by Congress on November 7, 1989, and signed by the President on November 8, 1989. The new law reinstates prior nondiscrimination rules applicable *before* the enactment of Section 89.

Section 89 created broad nondiscrimination requirements applicable to employer-sponsored health and group life insurance plans. However, its quantitative testing procedures proved overly complex and burdensome. Increasing frustration among employer groups and employee benefits practitioners resulted in the introduction of several measures aimed toward modification or outright repeal. Regulations issued by the Treasury Department this past March merely fueled the fire. Perhaps sensing an open revolt, Treasury repeatedly delayed the provision's effective date. On November 3, 1989, President Bush approved H.R. 2989, temporarily prohibiting the use of Treasury appropriations for the enforcement of Section 89.

The intent, and eventual demise, of Section 89 was succinctly addressed in the legislative history accompanying H.R.J. Reg 280:

Nondiscrimination in the provision of employer-provided health coverage remains an important policy objective, and the significant tax expenditures for employer-provided health coverage is justified only if such coverage does not discriminate in favor of highly compensated employees. However, the present-law nondiscrimination rules, or similar rules, are not at this time an appropriate way of achieving this objective. The present-law rules are overly complex and unduly burdensome on employers, and, therefore, it is appropriate to repeal the present-law section 89 rules.

Q. 321.2 What happened to the Section 89 nondiscrimination rules?

As a result of the repeal of Section 89, predecessor nondiscrimination rules for welfare benefit plans generally have been reinstated. Group term life insurance plans, self-insured medical plans, cafeteria plans per Section 125 of the Internal Revenue Code, dependent care plans, education reimbursement schemes, group legal services, and voluntary employee beneficiary associations (VEBAs) all fall under these earlier rules. On the other hand, there are now no nondiscrimination rules for *insured* medical plans. However, to reiterate, the old rules under Section 105(h) of the IRC are reinstated for *self-insured* medical plans. Under Section 105(h), a self-insured health care plan must not discriminate in favor of highly compensated individuals as to eligibility to participate or in terms of benefits provided.

Q. 322.1 What does "contingent workforce" mean and why is it of interest to legislators concerned with employee benefits?

The "contingent workforce" comprises the growing number of part-time and temporary employees filling jobs in the United States. Concerned members of the U.S. House of Representatives have proposed a "Part-Time and Temporary Workers Protection Act," aimed at requiring companies that use these so-called contingent workers to give them their fair share of core benefits, such as health and life insurance and pension plans. Although workforce flexibility is welcome in our economy, a bifurcated workforce is not. The fact that two-tiered wage provisions have lost their earlier luster in the unionized sector suggests that the groundswell will increase on behalf of minimum benefits for contingent workers. One survey showed 630,000 contingent workers in the temporary help industry alone, and discovered that only about one-fourth of them were getting employer-paid (at least in part) hospitalization and major medical insurance. And only about one-fifth were receiving life insurance.

Q. 357.1 Can benefit plans covered by the Employee Income Retirement Security Act (ERISA) be orally modified?

Oral modification of benefit plans has been rejected under ERISA. Under preempted state law, an employer used to be able to argue that if it made oral representations to an employee about benefits, the employee could not later deny or contradict those oral representations. But now, when ERISA applies, changes to a written plan must likewise be in writing.

Q. 369.1 Is the owner of a corporation automatically the alter ego of the company for pension payments?

During the past two years, a number of courts have considered whether an officer-shareholder or a related company can be held liable for a company's deficient pension contributions. In 1989, one U.S. appeals court ruled that the president and sole shareholder of a company in default on its pension funds was not personally liable to make up the deficiencies. Four multiemployer pension plans had sued the company for claimed arrearages. The corporation declared bankruptcy and a federal judge ruled that the president-sole shareholder had to pay up. The higher court overruled the judge, finding that neither the plain meaning nor the legislative history of ERISA calls for an alter-ego interpretation. (*Scarbrough v. Perez*, 870 F.2d 1079 (6th Cir. 1989))

Similarly the Court of Appeals for the Seventh Circuit held that former corporate officers of a defunct corporation could not be held personally liable, absent circumstances calling for "piercing the corporate veil," for delinquent contribution to plumbers union pension and welfare funds. (See, *Plumbers' Pensions Fund v. Niedrich*, No. 89-1015, 12/19/89.) However, this same court concluded differently in a case where the non-union half of a "double-breasted" trucking and excavating operation was found to be the alter ego of the unionized firm. The excavator's labor contract with the Teamsters required weekly pension contributions for three drivers. The owner first tried to talk the Teamsters into cancelling the contract out of business necessity. When the union refused, his wife started up the non-union firm and took over the hauling operations, and pension contributions stopped. Even though the new firm's trucking operations were later diversified, the court found it was started up only to avoid the pension obligations. Therefore, the court found one company to be the alter ego of the other and ordered it to bring the contributions current. (See *Central States Pension Fund v. Sloan*, No. 89-2355, 5/16/90.)

Q. 374.1 When does the statute of limitations begin to run on an ERISA claim by a pension?

In 1989, the U.S. Supreme Court refused to review a lower court's decision that the statute of limitations begins to run anew each time an employer sends a pensioner another incorrect pension check. The case involved retired General Vice President Frank Meagher of the International Association of Machinists. Meagher retired from the union in 1977 and sued in 1986, when the pension fund's trustees amended the plan to eliminate a "living pension" provision pegged to increases in staff salaries. (*Int'l Assoc. of Machinists v. Meagher*, No. 88-1427 (U.S. S. Ct., 4/24/89))

Q. 375.1 Can a creditor garnish an employee's welfare plan benefits?

Although ERISA does prevent creditors from garnishing or attaching an employee's pension benefits, the Supreme Court last year held that the same protection does not extend to other welfare benefit plans. (*Mackey v. Lawier Collections Agency and Service, Inc.*, 108 S. Ct. 218Z (1988)) In other words, if a creditor can garnish the money under a state garnishment statute, ERISA does not preempt such garnishment. For example, an employee's vacation or holiday pay is not protected from a garnishment order, even though ERISA clearly covers this benefit for other purposes.

Q. 385.1 Can a unionized employee, covered by a collective bargaining agreement, sue his or her employer if the company retaliates for the filing of a workers' compensation claim?

The U.S. Supreme Court recently resolved a dispute on this issue, which had divided many state and federal courts. Some courts felt that because the employee was covered by a collective bargaining agreement containing a grievance and arbitration procedure, the employee could not pursue a wrongful discharge claim. Instead, the employee had to either follow a grievance procedure or file a breach of contract claim pursuant to the collective bargaining agreement in federal court. Other courts had held that a unionized employee, just like a nonunion worker, should be allowed to file a tort claim challenging employee retaliation, particularly in states where the workers' compensation law did not contain a remedy for retaliation. The Supreme Court has now ruled unanimously that unionized, as well as nonunion workers, are entitled to pursue wrongful discharge and similar tort claims when they believe they have been punished by their employers for taking advantage of their workers' compensation rights. Of course, the Supreme Court decided only that federal law does not preempt state law in this respect. Relevant state common law must still recognize a tort cause of action on these kinds of facts; otherwise, the aggrieved employee may find that collective bargaining agreements contain the best remedies.

Q. 392 Must an employer provide employees with the option of joining a health maintenance organization?

A company must offer an HMO option if the following factors apply:

- The company offers a traditional health insurance plan;
- The company comes under the minimum-wage requirements of the federal Fair Labor Standards Act;
- During the previous calendar quarter, the company employed at least 25 workers; and
- The company receives a written request from a qualified HMO that covers a service area in which at least 25 of the company's employees live. These requirements are set by the Health Maintenance Organization Act. However, the employer is not required to pay more for health benefits as a result of offering a qualified HMO option than it would otherwise pay for health benefits under a collective bargaining agreement or other employer-employee contract in effect at the time the HMO is included in the health benefit plan.

Q. 406.1 Are there any circumstances under which an employer must offer benefits to nonemployees?

Yes, under the provisions of the Consolidated Omnibus Budget Reconciliation Act of 1986 (COBRA). This Act mandates group health insurance continuation coverage for employees and their dependents who would otherwise lose their group plan eligibility. Essentially, COBRA provides that when a "qualifying event" occurs, an employer must offer the affected covered employee and/or qualified beneficiary the option to continue to receive health coverage under the employer's group health plan. The coverage must be offered to the employee at a rate that does not exceed 102% of the total cost of providing coverage to similarly situated beneficiaries for whom a qualifying event has not occurred.

Q. 406.2 Which employers are subject to COBRA?

An employer that employs 20 or more persons on a typical business day and maintains a group health plan is required to provide continuation coverage. (Code Section 4980B(d))

Under new COBRA legislation, the definition of "employee" can include an independent contractor.

Q. 406.3 What is a "qualifying event"?

A qualifying event is any event that would normally result in a loss of coverage for the covered employee or qualified beneficiary were it not for the application of COBRA. These events are:

- The death of the covered employee;
- The termination (other than by reason of gross misconduct) or reduction of hours of the covered employee's employment;
- Divorce or legal separation;
- The covered employee's becoming entitled to Medicare benefits;
- A dependent child ceasing to meet dependency requirements; or
- A proceeding in a case under federal bankruptcy law with respect to the employer from whose employment the covered employee retired at any time. (Code Section 4980B(f)(3))

Q. 406.4 Who is required to receive continuation coverage when a qualifying event occurs?

Continuation coverage must be offered to any "covered employee" to whom a qualifying event occurs. A covered employee is any individual who is (or was) covered under a group health plan by virtue of that individual's employment or previous employment with the employer.

Continuation coverage must also be offered to any "qualified beneficiary." A qualified beneficiary is any individual who is (or was) a beneficiary under the plan as the spouse or the dependent child of the covered employee. Also, when the qualifying event is termination of employment or reduction of hours, a covered employee will be considered a qualified beneficiary. (Code Sections 4980B(f) and 4980B(g))

While an employer need not pay health care insurance costs for employees while they are on strike, strikers do not forfeit their COBRA rights. They are entitled to notice and opportunity to continue their group health insurance at their own expense. Furthermore, according to the court, the 45-day grace period for the initial premium payment could not be shortened by New York Telephone in the case of its striking workers. (See *Communications Workers of America v. NYNEX Corp.*, 12 EBC Cases 1049 (2d Cir. 3/16/90).)

Q. 406.5 How long must the continuation coverage last?

Generally, continuation coverage must last at least 36 months. However, when the coverage is triggered by a termination of employment or a reduction of hours, continuation coverage must last only 18 months. If a second qualifying event occurs before expiration of this 18-month period, the period is extended to 36 months. The above notwithstanding, coverage can also be terminated when the qualified beneficiary becomes covered by another group health plan or eligible for Medicare benefits. (Code Section 4980B(f)(2)(B))

However, COBRA continuation need not end, when the beneficiary becomes covered by a new employer's plan, if the new plan excludes preexisting medical conditions. This change in the law took effect for qualifying events occurring after December 31, 1989, and for people who elected COBRA coverage after December 31, 1988—or who tried to pay and were rejected. Effective since mid-December '89, a COBRA amendment allows workers on Social Security disability benefits to stretch COBRA coverage another 11 months, for a total of 29 months of eligibility. Additionally, if an employee becomes eligible for Medicare during the 18-month COBRA eligibility period, any beneficiary under the COBRA coverage can continue it for 36 months from the date of the employee's entitlement for Medicare benefits.

Q. 406.6 What are the various notice requirements under COBRA?

When an employee begins coverage under a group health plan, written notice of COBRA rights must be given to the employee and his or her spouse. If a qualifying event occurs (other than a change in dependency status of a child, a divorce, or a legal separation) the employer is required to give notice to the plan administrator within 30 days of the qualifying event. In the event of divorce or legal separation, or when a child ceases to be a dependent, the covered employee or qualified beneficiary must notify the plan administrator within 60 days of such event. Within 14 days of receipt of that notice, the plan administrator must notify the covered employee and/or qualified beneficiary of his or her COBRA rights. (Code Section 4908B(f)(6))

Q. 406.7 What are the sanctions for failure to comply with COBRA?

An employer will be assessed a tax of $100 per day for each failure to properly notify a qualified beneficiary of his or her COBRA rights. (The tax for failure with respect to family coverage is $200 per day per family.) The noncompliance period may extend six months after the date on which the continuation coverage could be terminated. For example, if an employee is terminated, and the employer failed to provide the COBRA notice, the noncompliance period would be 24 months (18 months continuation for terminated employees plus 6 months). Under certain circumstances, a third party that administers the health plan for the employer may be held liable for this tax.

No excise tax will be assessed if the failure (1) is not the result of willful neglect, and (2) is corrected within 30 days. Furthermore, there is an aggregate dollar limit on the tax when the failure is due to reasonable cause. This limit is equal to the lesser of (1) 10% of aggregate cost the employer pays or incurs in providing for health coverage or (2) $500,000. Finally, if it is shown that the failure would not have been discovered by an employer exercising reasonable diligence, no tax will be imposed. (Code Sections 4980B(c) and 4980B(f))

Q. 406.8 What is the federal income tax status of employer-provided educational assistance?

Prior to changes in the tax law in 1988, payments to employees of up to $5,250 per year for tuition, fees, books, supplies, and so forth could be excluded from gross income under an employer's educational assistance program. (Code Section 127) For tax years beginning after 1988, however, tax-free treatment of payments under an educational assistance program is not available. Educational assistance that is not excludable under other Code sections, for example, Section 117 (qualified scholarships), Section 132 (employee fringe benefits), or Section 162 (trade-or-business expenses), is includible in gross income and subject to federal income tax and employment taxes.

Section 117 excludes from gross income scholarships which degree candidates at certain qualified educational organizations receive, and amounts that are qualified tuition reductions which employees of educational institutions receive. Section 132 extends the Section 117 exclusion for employee tuition reduction amounts to a broader range of individuals, including the spouses and dependent children of employees of educational institutions, retired and disabled employees, and surviving spouses of employees of educational institutions.

Section 162 excludes from an employee's gross income tuition assistance for certain job-related education. To qualify as job-related, a course must maintain or improve skills required for an employee's current job, or be required as a condition of continuing employment in a current job. Courses that prepare an employee for a new trade or business or courses that an employee needs to meet a job's minimum educational requirements do not qualify.

Q. 406.9 How are dependent care expenses treated for federal income tax purposes?

Two forms of tax relief are generally available to taxpayers who pay dependent care expenses. The dependent care credit enables individuals to reduce their federal tax by a credit equal to a sliding percentage (30%–20%, based on adjusted gross income) of dependent care expenses to a maximum of $2,400 (in expenses) for one dependent and $4,800 for two or more dependents. (Congress is considering a proposal that would increase the dependent care credit to 34% for taxpayers with adjusted gross incomes of at least $8,000, but less than $10,000. The proposal would also make the credit refundable for certain taxpayers.) A dependent care assistance plan enables individuals to exclude from income as much as $5,000 of child care expenses paid or reimbursed through the plan. Amounts excluded from income under a dependent care assistance program (DCAP) will directly offset the annual dollar limit for qualifying expenses that can be taken into account in calculating the dependent care tax credit.

Q. 406.10 What is a DCAP?

A DCAP is a written nondiscriminatory plan pursuant to which an employer provides to an employee on a tax-free basis child or dependent care services. The amount excludable from gross income is limited to $5,000 ($2,500 for married individuals filing separately). Furthermore, the amount excluded from the employee's income in any taxable year cannot exceed the employee's earned income for the taxable year or, if the employee is married at the end of the year, the lesser of the employee's or the spouse's earned income.

To claim the exclusion, an employee is generally required to include on his or her tax return the name, address, and taxpayer identification number of the person performing the child or dependent care services.

Amounts that are excluded from gross income under a DCAP will directly offset dependent care expenses that could otherwise be available for purposes of the dependent care credit.

Q. 406.11 What is the dependent care tax credit?

Code Section 21 provides an income tax credit with respect to dependent care expenses a taxpayer incurs in order to be gainfully employed. The dependent care expenses must be incurred with respect to a "qualifying individual," which is defined as a dependent under age 13 for whom the taxpayer can claim a dependency exemption, a dependent who is physically or mentally incapable of caring for himself or herself, or the taxpayer's spouse if he or she is physically or mentally incapable of caring for himself or herself.

Taxpayers with adjusted gross incomes of $10,000 or less are allowed a credit equal to 30% of employment-related expenses. (Modifications are currently being considered by Congress as discussed in 409.6.) For taxpayers with adjusted gross incomes of from $10,000 to $28,000, the credit is reduced by one percentage point for each $2,000 of adjusted gross income, or fraction thereof, above $10,000. The employment-related expenses that will qualify for the credit may not exceed the employee's earned income for a taxable year, or, if the employee is married at the end of the year, the lesser of the employee's or the spouse's earned income. These expenses are further limited to $2,400 per year ($4,800 for two or more qualifying dependents). Furthermore, the credit is unavailable for any qualifying dependent care expenses for which payments or reimbursements have been made by an employer under a DCAP.

Q. 406.12 What is new in the area of family leave laws?

On the federal front, a family leave act neared passage as this Supplement went to press, under a threat from President Bush to veto it. (See "Pending Legislation," Appendix B.)

New Jersey joined those states, e.g., California and Montana, that have enacted their own family leave acts. Some of the guidelines issued by New Jersey with respect to its new law are reprinted below; they are a good illustration of approximately what's in store for all of us eventually.

> **Legislative findings and declarations.** The Legislature finds and declares that the number of families in the State in which both parents or a single parent is employed outside of the home has increased dramatically and continues to increase and that due to lack of employment policies to accommodate working parents, many individuals are forced to choose between job security and parenting or providing care for ill family members. The Legislature further finds that it is necessary to promote the economic security of families by guaranteeing jobs to wage earners who

choose to take a period of leave upon the birth or placement for adoption of a child or serious health condition of a family member. The Legislature, therefore, declares that it is the policy of the State to protect and promote the stability and economic security of family units. The Legislature further declares that employees should be entitled to take a period of leave upon the birth or placement for adoption of a child or serious health condition of a family member without the risk of termination of employment or retaliation by employers and without loss of certain benefits.

The New Jersey laws provide that an employee is entitled to a family leave of 12 weeks in any 24-month period upon advance notice to the employer. The family leave may be paid, unpaid, or a combination. The employer may require that any period of family leave be supported by certification issued by a duly licensed health care provider. The employer may deny family leave if (1) the employee is a salaried employee who is among the highest paid 5% of the employer's workforce, or among the seven highest paid employees, (2) the denial is necessary to prevent "substantial and grievous" economic injury to the employer's operations, and (3) the employer notifies the employee of its intent to deny the leave at the time the employer determines that the denial is necessary.

Q. 406.13 What is the status of the Medicare Catastrophic Coverage Act?

The Medicare Catastrophic Coverage Act was signed by President Ronald Reagan in July 1988. The idea was to protect older Americans from financial ruin resulting from long term, acute illnesses. The Act expanded coverage for hospital stays and skilled nursing, plus prescription drugs and a ceiling on out-of-pocket costs for doctor bills. The reaction of the intended beneficiaries was anger and outrage. Senior citizens simply refused to accept the income tax surcharge intended to finance these new benefits. Despite the fact that maintenance-of-effort obligations, imposed upon employers by the Act, would have resulted in refunds of tax to at least some retirees, vehement criticism and cries for repeal led Congress to repeal the entire program on November 22, 1989.

Executive Compensation

Q. 424.1 Are retired executives taxed on their life insurance premiums?

The changes introduced by the Tax Reform Act of 1986 (TRA '86) set forth that an executive over age 65 will be taxed on the full cost of his or her permanent group life insurance coverage. (IRC Section 79(d)(1)(B)) Because of this, employers will be barred from providing employer-purchased excess group insurance that discriminates in favor of key executives and retirees. An executive covered by a discriminatory life insurance policy will show imputed income in an increasingly larger amount each year.

Q. 431 What are stock depreciation rights?

Stock depreciation rights compensate option holders when the stock price falls. The Securities and Exchange Commission (SEC) requires corporate insiders to hold stock for at least six months before exercising stock options. Stock depreciation rights make up for the difference between the stock market value at the end of that six-month period and the exercise price. The employer pays the executive the difference in cash.

Q. 431.1 What is the accounting treatment of stock depreciation rights?

The emerging issues task force of the Financial Accounting Standards Board (FASB) has ruled that, for accounting purposes, as long as the stock depreciation rights cover the six-month period and are limited to corporate insiders, the compensation expense begins only when the related option is exercised, and only to the extent that the market price declines below the exercise date level.

Q. 441.1 How can an employer modify a Section 422A incentive stock option plan?

In the event of a stock dividend or split, a shareholder receives a pro rata increase in the number of shares held while the market price of a share decreases proportionately. To correct this in respect to option holders, a corresponding adjustment is necessary to increase the number of shares subject to the options and to adjust the exercise price so the holders' position remains the same relative to the shareholders' position.

In a recent private letter ruling, IRS held that such adjustment in the exercise price and number of options is not necessary in the case of a cash dividend and a distribution of debentures, because the shareholders receive no additional ownership interest in the corporation, and the option holders benefit from the greater number of shares against which they can exercise their options.

Therefore, if a corporation adjusts the exercise price and increases the number of options as a consequence of a cash and subordinated debentures distribution, IRS will probably find that the adjustment constitutes a modification of the incentive stock option (ISO) plan under IRC Section 425(h); as such, it will be deemed to be a grant of new options.

IRS also held that if the exercise price of the outstanding options after the modification is less than the stock fair market value on the date of the modification, the options will cease to qualify as ISOs under IRC Section 422A and will be taxable under IRC Section 83 as nonqualified options.

Q. 463 Who are highly compensated employees under TRA '86?

TRA '86 set forth antidiscrimination rules that apply to various types of plans. These antidiscrimination provisions tend to deny tax benefits to highly compensated employees who qualify under plans that discriminate in their favor. The definition of "highly compensated employee" can be found at IRS Temp. Reg. §1.414(q)-IT, issued in February 1988.

A highly compensated *active* employee is generally a person who:

(1) Is an officer and who makes more than $45,000 (as indexed) per year;

(2) Makes more than $75,000 (as indexed) per year;

(3) Owns more than 5% of the employer; or

(4) Is both in the top-paid 20% of the employer's employees and makes more than $50,000 (as indexed) per year.

Former employees who were highly compensated when they terminated employment or in any year ending after they attained age 55 are generally treated as highly compensated *former* employees. Both active and former employees form an employer's roster of highly compensated employees in regard to a given plan. (See Questions 321.1, 321.9–321.14, and 321.18.)

Q. 463.1 What are the testing periods for determining who is a highly compensated employee?

The first step in determining who is a highly compensated employee is to identify the relevant testing period. In general, testing is done based on the current plan year and the current plan year plus the preceding 12-month period.

Q. 463.2 Are there any other considerations in determining who is a highly compensated employee?

Once an employee identifies the relevant testing period, it uses the procedure below to determine who qualifies as a highly compensated employee. An employer must determine:

(1) Who is the employee's employer during the relevant testing period;

(2) Who is an employee;

(3) The employee's compensation;

(4) The size of the top-paid group;

(5) Who is a highly compensated active employee in the look-back year;

(6) Who is a highly compensated active employee in the determination year; and

(7) Who is a highly compensated former employee.

An employer needs to determine who is a highly compensated employee because it will want to choose the optimal alternative when it decides whether to make a given election in applying the nondiscrimination rules to plans such as medical insurance, qualified retirement, group life insurance, cafeteria plans, and so forth.

Q. 463.3 Can an employer contribute to a pension plan to provide medical benefits for retirees?

Under a change in the law, companies can contribute into so-called 401(h) accounts up to 25% of aggregate pension contributions to fund retiree health and life insurance. Since the new law requires the contribution to be calculated as a factor of pension fund contributions, no 401(h) account contributions can be made if the pension plan is already fully funded.

Q. 464.1 Are there any limits on benefit payouts from defined-benefit retirement plans?

TRA '86 created new limits on the maximum amount a defined-benefit retirement plan may pay out. For example, companies may no longer accrue for and pay early retirement benefits beyond the following figures:

(1) Up to retirement age 55, the maximum payout is $40,000;

(2) Up to retirement age 60, the maximum payout is $60,200;

(3) Up to retirement age 62, the maximum payout is $72,000; and

(4) Up to retirement age 65, the maximum payout is $90,000.

(These caps are indexed for inflation.) Social Security retirement age and other factors can affect payout figures.

Q. 464.2 What cash-or-deferred arrangements are permitted under a 401(k) plan?

Under a 401(k) plan, employees may, under certain conditions, make pretax contributions to qualified profit-sharing and stock bonus plans. Section 401(k) contains nondiscrimination rules that peg the allowable amount of salary deduction deferrals highly compensated employees may make to the level of such deferrals nonhighly compensated employees make for the year, expressed as a percentage of their compensation (the actual deferral percentage (ADP)). On August 8, 1988, IRS published final and proposed regulations (Prop. Reg. §1.401(k)) regarding cash-or-deferred arrangements. In addition to providing new formulas for calculating ADPs for plan years after 1986 (to conform with the changes brought by TRA '86, the final regulations incorporate several of the less controversial aspects of TRA '86 with respect to 401(k) plans.

The changes provide that:

(1) Section 401(k) will be the exclusive means of providing for the deferral of employees' contributions in a qualified plan;

(2) Employees will be taxed on any amounts deferred into a qualified plan, even if deferral is made before the end of the year in which the compensation is earned or available, if the plan does not satisfy the requirements of Section 401(k);

(3) Only profit-sharing, stock bonus, and certain other special arrangements will be permitted to contain Section 401(k) provisions; and

(4) Elective deferrals will be treated as plan assets for purposes of applying the Employee Retirement Income Security Act (ERISA) requirement that all plan assets be held in trust and be subject to Title I of ERISA.

Q. 464.3 What are considered valid elective employee contributions in regard to IRC Section 401(k)?

To be considered valid elective employee contributions, the final regulations indicate that the elective contributions must:

(1) Be allocated to the employees' accounts under this plan within the plan year;

(2) Actually be paid to the trust no later than the end of the 12-month period immediately following the plan year to which the contribution relates; and

(3) Relate to compensation that either would have been received by the employee during the plan year or is attributable to services performed by the employee in the plan year and would have been received by the employee within the 2½ months after the close of that year absent the election to defer.

One-time irrevocable elections an employee makes upon commencement of employment or upon initial eligibility will not be treated as cash-or-deferred elections under IRC Section 401(k).

Q. 464.4 Are there any limits on how much an executive may contribute to a 401(k) plan?

TRA '86 reduced the maximum allowable annual contribution to Section 401(k) savings plans from $30,000 to about $7,600 a year. (IRC Section 402(g)(1)) Therefore, the amount of income an executive can defer each year has been greatly reduced. Executives are faced with increased taxes because they can no longer defer current income and lose the long-term deferral on earnings.

Q. 464.5 What happens to IRA contributions in the wake of TRA '86?

After TRA '86, the annual IRA contribution of $2,000 is eliminated for most executives. (IRC Sections 415(b)(2)(c) and 415(b)(2)(d))

Q. 464.6 What limits have been placed on hardship distributions from a 401(k) plan?

Commencing in 1989, hardship distributions under a 401(k) plan are limited to the amount of an employee's elective deferral. The income attributable to those elective deferrals may no longer be withdrawn.

Q. 468.1 Are severance payments subject to ERISA?

If a severance payment agreement is reclassified to be subject to ERISA regulations, it must comply with ERISA requirements, which may mean that:

- The employer will be subject to fines by the Department of Labor for failure to file a Form 5500 for the plan or for failure to disclose information about the plan to participants; and
- The employees will be classified as plan participants with rights under ERISA (thus exposing the employer to lawsuits under ERISA if it denies severance payments).

An ERISA fund, program, or plan implies:

- Intended benefits;
- Intended beneficiaries;
- A source of financing; and
- A procedure to apply for and collect benefits.

Therefore, it seems that a severance payment agreement incorporating these four features can be characterized as an employee benefit plan under ERISA, subject to reporting, disclosure, and fiduciary responsibility requirements. (*Holland v. Burlington Industries, Inc.*, 772 F.2d 1140 (1985), and *Scott v. Gulf Oil Corp.*, 754 F.2d 1499 (1985))

In addition to ERISA coverage, severance plans also continue to be challenged in the area of discrimination. (See Question 233.3.) Thus, employers must consider not only ERISA, but also the Age Discrimination in Employment Act (ADEA) in structuring and applying severance plans. In particular, there is sometimes an interplay between severance and early retirement plans in plant-closing situations. As the law is developing, it seems that employers in such situations can structure these dove-tailed plans so that older employees can get the benefit of one, but not both, such programs. (See *EEOC v. Chrysler Corp.*, 89 Civ. 1347, S.D.N.Y., 1/31/90.)

Q. 468.2 Are golden parachute agreements subject to ERISA?

In general, golden parachute agreements are not subject to the ERISA regulations applicable to other severance payments. However, in December 1988 a district court held an individual employment agreement providing severance benefits to the corporation's top executives to be subject to ERISA, because it found the definition of severance pay plan to include golden parachute agreements. (*Purser v. Enron*, No. 881117 (D. W. Pa. 12/5/88)) Employers should use extreme care when structuring golden parachute agreements to ensure that the agreements do not come under the definition of an ERISA plan.

Q. 468.3 When can a severance payment avoid ERISA reclassification?

The U.S. Supreme Court has established that the employer's obligation to pay a single one-time, lump-sum payment to each individual within a certain class triggered by a one-time occurrence cannot be classified as a benefit plan that subjects the employer to ERISA compliance. (*Fort Halifax Packaging Co. v. Coyne*, 107 S. Ct. 2211 (1987)) Therefore, an employer can regard as safe a single set of severance payments due upon the occurrence of a certain event.

Q. 479.1 What is the golden parachute rule?

The golden parachute rule provides that any excess parachute payment:

- Is not deductible by the corporate payor (IRC Section 280G(a)); and
- Subjects the recipient to a nondeductible 20% excise tax (IRC Section 4999(a)).

Q. 479.2 Are there any exemptions from the definition of parachute payment?

TRA '86 exempts from the definition of parachute payment any payment:

(1) Made to (or for the benefit of) a disqualified individual with regard to a corporation that was a small business corporation immediately before the change in control or ownership;
(2) Made to (or for the benefit of) a disqualified individual with regard to a corporation the stock of which was not readily tradable on an established securities market or otherwise immediately before the change in control, and the shareholders approved such payment (the no-market exemption);
(3) From or to a qualified pension, profit-sharing, or stock bonus plan (IRC Section 401(a)), including a tax-exempt trust under IRC Section 501(a);
(4) From or to a qualified annuity plan (IRC Section 403(a));
(5) From or to a simplified employee pension plan (IRC Section 408(k));
(6) Any portion of which the taxpayer establishes by clear and convincing evidence is reasonable compensation for personal services to be rendered on or after the change in ownership or control (IRC Section 280G(b)(4)(A)).

These exempted payments are not taken into account in determining whether the 300% threshold test (see Questions 485–488 in the main volume) for a parachute payment has been met. (IRC Section 280G(b)(2))

Q. 479.3 When is the no-market exemption unavailable?

The no-market exemption may be unavailable to corporations that have no tradable stock if a substantial portion of any other entity's assets consist (directly or indirectly) of stock in the no-market corporation making the payment and any of the other entity's interests trade on an established securities market or otherwise.

Q. 479.4 Is the business judgment rule applied to assess golden parachutes?

Recently, the California Court of Appeals applied the business judgment rule to approve golden parachute agreements a target company's outside directors set up for the company's senior executives. (*Gaillard v. Natomas Co.*, A040647 (Cal. Ct. App. 3/23/89)) The rule was not applied, however, to the judicial review of the inside directors' conduct, because the court deemed that the inside directors were not performing directorial duties in seeking approval of the golden parachutes and accepting benefits under the agreements.

Q. 496.1 Are distributions from qualified pension plans ever taxed?

Yes. Pursuant to IRC Section 4981A(a), a 15% excise tax is imposed on distributions from all types of qualified plans (qualified savings plans, IRA plans, profit-sharing plans, defined-benefit plans) when the distributions exceed $117,529 in the aggregate.

Q. 498.1 What are some common nonqualified plans?

- Supplemental executive retirement programs (SERPs);
- Rabbi trusts;
- Secular trusts;
- Nonqualified annuity plans;
- Nonqualified stock option plans;
- Top-hat plans; and
- Deferred-bonus arrangements.

Q. 498.2 What is a nonqualified stock option plan?

Stock option plans that are not addressed by IRC Sections 421–425 are considered nonqualified stock option plans. After receipt of a stock option, an employee may select the year in which it will be treated as taxable income. Tax may be incurred: (1) upon receipt of the option, (2) when the option is exercised, (3) when any valid restrictions on disposition of the stock lapse, or (4) when the stock is actually disposed of. The employer is entitled to a deduction for the amount the employee is required to include in income.

Q. 498.3 What is a funded plan?

In a funded plan, contributions are irrevocably placed outside the employer's reach. Such plans are commonly funded through trusts or annuity contracts. Even though the trust contains funds that will eventually be distributed to employees, the employees are not treated as the owners of the trust. However, if the level of employee contributions to the trust exceeds the level of employer contributions, the trust is treated as owned by the employee and earned income is taxable.

Tax deferral in a nonqualified plan generally derives from a deferral of vesting. Thus, as long as unrestricted rights to the benefits are contingent upon an event (e.g., reaching a specified number of years of service), tax on such benefits may be deferred.

Q. 498.4 How are nonqualified plans treated under ERISA?

ERISA provides general rules applicable to employee benefits plans. It also contains certain rules that mirror the qualification standards expressed in the Internal Revenue Code (e.g., participation, vesting, and funding requirements). Generally, these rules will not apply to nonqualified plans. However, ERISA also provides guidance relating to fiduciary obligations and reporting and disclosure requirements. These provisions may be imposed on nonqualified plans. The extent to which ERISA pertains will vary depending upon the type of nonqualified plan.

Q. 504 Can deferred compensation be funded by nonqualified deferred annuity contracts?

An employer can fund deferred compensation by buying an annuity contract issued to the employee and providing restrictions on transferability. The value of the premiums the employer pays is included in the employee's gross income (therefore, income credited to the cash value will not be subject to current tax), and the amount made available to the employee is deferred until the year it is paid.

Q. 511.1 What is a secular trust?

Secular trusts are so named to distinguish them from rabbi trusts. Unlike a rabbi trust, the employer contribution to the secular trust and the earnings thereon are taxable to the employee. Also, a secular trust is subject to the reporting and disclosure requirements of ERISA. The major advantage of a secular trust over a rabbi trust is that monies held in secular trusts cannot be reached by creditors of the employer.

Q. 512.1 Have rabbi trust arrangements with hardship withdrawal provisions been approved?

In recent private letter rulings, IRS has allowed hardship withdrawals in connection with rabbi trusts, thus allowing greater flexibility in structuring nonqualified deferred-compensation and rabbi trusts. Withdrawals are permitted for unforeseeable emergencies (for example, severe financial hardship to the participant or beneficiary, loss of participant or beneficiary's property due to casualty) arising from events beyond the participant's or beneficiary's control. If the plan provides for payment of the benefit in the form of a life annuity at retirement, the accrued benefit may be made available if an unforseeable emergency occurs.

Similarly, withdrawals are also allowed for emergencies before retirement (for example, cases of hardship occurring during employment and that cannot be relieved otherwise).

In both cases, hardship withdrawals are limited to the reasonable amount needed to satisfy the emergency.

The employer is not adversely affected by hardship withdrawals because contributions to rabbi trusts are taxed when the participant receives distributions from the trust. The employer may deduct the contributions when the participant includes the distributions in income.

Q. 513.1 How can rabbi trusts be funded?

Employers must choose rabbi trust assets carefully. Employer's stock, life insurance, and annuity contracts should be excluded because of the tax implications.

Q. 513.2 When are contributions to rabbi trusts deductible?

Generally, IRS treats rabbi trusts as unfunded promises to pay deferred compensation. In one private letter ruling, however, IRS hinted that rabbi trusts might be treated as funded for purposes of IRC Section 404(a)(5). If that position prevails, the employer will have to maintain separate accounts to obtain a deduction for its contribution to the trust.

Q. 513.3 How can employer securities be used in rabbi trusts?

Rabbi trusts have been treated as unfunded for ERISA purposes in numerous private letter rulings because the funds are within reach of the employer's creditors if the employer experiences financial difficulty.

IRS considers employer securities inappropriate assets to hold in a rabbi trust. If employer securities are used, IRS requires examination of state law issues to determine what the employee's, employer's, and creditors' rights to the employer securities would be. If, for example, the security is treated as treasury stock under state law, then presumably the trust would be considered unfunded. Furthermore, problems may arise under IRC Section 83 if the employee has the right to vote the employer securities held in the rabbi trust.

Q. 520.1 Are top-hat plans exempt from plan asset regulations?

The Department of Labor (DOL) has issued final regulations (29 CFR 2510.3-102) that require employee contributions to qualified plans to be placed in trust as soon as practicable after they are contributed, but in no event more than 90 days after the employer receives the funds. Employers are concerned that this rule would require the funding of executive deferred-compensation plans that are maintained on a salary reduction basis and, therefore, would eliminate the use of the top-hat exemption, which requires that the plan be unfunded. This may be avoided if DOL exempts bona fide top-hat plans from the plan asset regulations.

Q. 522 What is a supplemental executive retirement program (SERP)?

A SERP is a nonqualified program that is funded by corporate-owned insurance. The tax-free build-up of life insurance contracts provides important benefits, because the company can completely recover its cost from insurance proceeds. The company benefits that employees receive after retirement are 100% tax deductible. IRS approval is not required, because the program is not subject to IRS rules. Most important, employers can freely choose which executives will participate and determine benefits to participants on a discriminatory basis without violating any equal employment or ERISA laws.

The ting of the executive's income and the employer's tax deductions is governed by the same rules that apply to excess-benefits plans. If a SERP does not qualify as a top-hat plan, all five parts of Title I of ERISA apply to the plan. (See Questions 519 and 521 in the main volume.)

Job Safety

Q. 528.1 What is a worksite analysis?

The purpose of worksite analysis is to identify hazards. Employers may conduct worksite safety and health surveys; analyses of facilities, processes, materials, and equipment; and routine job hazard analyses to identify hazards. Elements of this analysis include regular safety and health inspections, a system through which employees can notify management about potential hazards without fear of reprisal, investigation of accidents and averted accidents, and identification of injury and illness trends with common causes.

Q. 528.2 How can hazards be prevented or controlled?

To prevent or control current or potential hazards identified by the employer, the Occupational Safety and Health Administration (OSHA) guidelines recommend establishing procedures using engineering techniques, safe work training, provision of personal protective equipment, and administrative controls. Other than procedural safeguards, the guidelines suggest employers maintain facilities and equipment, plan and prepare for emergencies, and establish a medical program including on-site first-aid and nearby emergency medical care.

Q. 528.3 What should safety and health training encompass?

The OSHA guidelines note that information employees need will vary but that each employee should at least be informed about the general hazards and safety rules of the worksite; specific hazards, safety rules, and practices related to particular work assignments; and actions the employee should take in the event of an emergency.

Safety and health training of supervisors should include the information employees need as well as information about safety and health management responsibilities.

Q. 529.1 Does the Occupational Safety and Health Administration have any regulations involving shutdown of equipment while under repair?

In mid-1988, OSHA issued its long-awaited rules on lockout/tagout procedures to prevent the unexpected energizing, start up, or energy release of equipment that is shut down for repair or maintenance. According to OSHA, in many industries 10% of serious accidents may be prevented by these regulations. Experienced labor, personal injury, and product liability lawyers agree that a frequent source of injuries and lawsuits is absence of fail-safe devices to shut down machinery during unjamming or similar activities. OSHA estimates 122 fatalities and 60,000 injuries will now be avoided each year.

Q. 529.2 What are the major elements of an effective occupational safety and health program under OSHA?

According to the guidelines, an effective occupational safety and health program includes four elements: (1) management commitment and employee involvement, (2) worksite analysis, (3) hazard prevention and control, and (4) safety and health training.

Q. 529.3 What measures can an employer take to ensure management commitment and employee involvement?

To ensure management commitment and employee involvement, the OSHA guidelines recommend that employers:

(1) Articulate a worksite policy on safety and health;

(2) Establish a clear goal for the program and identify objectives to meet the goal;

(3) Make visible the involvement of top management in implementing the program;

(4) Encourage employee involvement in the structure and operation of the program and in decisions that affect their safety and health;

(5) Divide all program responsibilities among management, supervisors, and employees;

(6) Provide adequate authority and resources to individuals with program responsibilities;

(7) Make individuals with program responsibilities accountable; and

(8) Review program operations annually.

Q. 529.4 Does OSHA provide any voluntary guidelines for employers seeking to improve their employees' working conditions?

Yes. In January 1989, OSHA issued voluntary guidelines that are appropriate for most employers. The guidelines are designed to encourage management practices that will prevent occupational injuries and illnesses. OSHA advises employers to establish comprehensive occupational safety and health programs that provide systematic policies, procedures, and practices. The OSHA voluntary guidelines do not apply to employers in the construction industry.

Q. 563.1 May an employer whose conduct does not meet OSHA requirements be subject to penalties other than those provided by OSHA?

In February 1989, the Illinois Supreme Court—the highest court yet to consider the question—ruled that OSHA does not prevent the state from prosecuting an employer under state criminal laws for conduct that was also regulated by OSHA and federal law. The court based its decision in *Illinois v. Chicago Magnet Wire Corp.* (Ill. Sup. Ct., Dkt. No. 65588) on the fact that OSHA encourages the states to develop their own occupational safety and health plans. The court noted that criminal charges do not impose new responsibilities on employers, but instead impose additional sanctions for improper conduct that "threatens or results in serious physical injury or death to workers." According to the court, state penal sanctions would serve as retribution, as well as a deterrent, keeping employers from violating safety standards. The Illinois Supreme Court decision has spurred prosecutors in other states to plan criminal prosecutions of OSHA violators. The Illinois Supreme Court's decision was in agreement with the Department of Justice position on the issue.

Q. 565 Have any states instituted their own OSHA-type programs?

Connecticut legislators are planning to introduce in Congress the Construction, Safety, Health and Education Act of 1989 in May of 1989, which would provide for the criminal prosecution of negligent employers engaged in the construction industry.

Q. 567.1 Has OSHA's hazard communication standard been extended beyond the manufacturing sector?

Late in 1988, the Third Circuit Court of Appeals in Philadelphia, which had earlier ordered OSHA to extend its regulations beyond the manufacturing sector, approved OSHA's expanded standard. In doing so, the court lifted an earlier stay that had prevented OSHA from applying that standard to companies in the construction industry.

Q. 570.1 Has OSHA made any changes in chemical exposure limits during the past year?

In what some observers describe as the agency's most significant rulemaking to date, OSHA, in 1989, lowered the permissible exposure limits for about 400 chemicals. The exposure limits were reduced based on recommendations by the American Conference of Governmental Industrial Hygienists and the National Institute of Occupational Safety and Health (NIOSH). The recommendations reflect newly available medical and health information.

Many larger manufacturing and chemical companies have reported little anticipated impact because they claim to already be complying with analogous standards of the American Conference of Governmental Industrial Hygienists. In contrast, smaller companies, such as family owned firms, may have some trouble meeting the more stringent limits. The new rules cover many of the most common workplace chemicals, including chloroform, carbon monoxide, hydrogen cyanide, and wood dust. The standards became effective March 1, 1989, but allowed for a six-month phase-in period. Employers can comply with the new limits by using a combination of controls, including engineering, workplace practices, and respiratory protection.

Currently OSHA lacks an automatic review mechanism that would allow the limits to reflect scientific data as they become available. Without such a mechanism, periodic reviews are required. One problem with a system requiring periodic reviews is that, until the reviews are made and revisions implemented, OSHA will contain some standards that are outdated and unsafe.

Q. 577.1 Is any of the information from completed material safety data sheets (MSDSs), emergency and hazardous chemical inventory forms, or toxic release forms available to the public?

Yes. Information from MSDSs is available to the public upon request to the local emergency planning committee. Information from emergency and hazardous chemical inventory forms is available to the public upon written request to the local emergency planning committee or state emergency response commission. Information from toxic chemical release forms is available to the public from the administrator of the Environmental Protection Agency (EPA), who is responsible for maintaining a national toxic chemical inventory computer database. (See also Questions 578.1–578.17 below.)

Q. 578.1 What is the purpose of the Emergency Planning and Community Right to Know Act?

The Emergency Planning and Community Right to Know Act (42 U.S.C. §§11001–11050 (1986)) is designed to avert catastrophe if unacceptable levels of hazardous substances are released into the environment. The Act mandates decentralized emergency planning and institutes reporting requirements.

Q. 578.2 What emergency planning measures are mandated by the Emergency Planning and Community Right to Know Act?

The Act calls for states to establish state emergency response commissions, emergency planning districts, and local emergency planning committees. The Act requires states to prepare comprehensive emergency response plans. The Act also requires emergency and emergency planning notification. Additionally, the Act includes provisions for emergency training and emergency system review.

Q. 578.3 How are state emergency response commissions, emergency planning districts, and local emergency planning committees established?

The governor of each state appoints members to a state emergency response commission. Appointees should have technical expertise in the emergency response field, if practicable. The state emergency response commission designates emergency planning districts and appoints members to emergency planning committees.

Q. 578.4 What are the responsibilities of the state emergency response commissions?

State emergency response commissions must designate emergency planning districts, appoint local emergency planning committees, supervise and coordinate the activities of the local emergency planning committees, establish procedures for receiving and processing public requests for information, and designate an information coordinator.

Q. 578.5 Who must be included in local emergency planning committees?

Local emergency planning committees must include representatives from the fields of law enforcement, civil defense, firefighting, first aid, and health; local environmental, hospital, and transportation personnel; members of the broadcast and print media and community groups; representatives of state and local officials; and owners and operators of facilities that use extremely hazardous substances.

Q. 578.6 How many local emergency planning committees must be established?

One local emergency planning committee must be established for each emergency planning district.

Q. 578.7 What are the responsibilities of the local emergency planning committees?

Local emergency planning committees must prepare comprehensive emergency response plans, review the plans annually or as required by changed circumstances, establish procedures for receiving and processing public requests for information, and designate an information coordinator.

Q. 578.8 What emergency planning notification is required by the Emergency Planning and Community Right to Know Act?

The Act requires owners or operators of facilities that have extremely hazardous substances in excess of the established threshold to notify the facility's state emergency response commission that the facility is subject to the requirements of the Act.

Q. 578.9 What provisions must be included in emergency response plans?

Emergency response plans must include provisions that identify facilities subject to the requirements of the Act within the emergency planning district, routes used for the transportation of extremely hazardous substances, and risk facilities near facilities subject to the requirements of the Act. Plans must also include: (1) response procedures to be followed in the event of a release of extremely hazardous substances; (2) provisions for designating community and facility emergency coordinators; (3) notification procedures the coordinators must follow to inform a designated individual and the public that a release has occurred; (4) methods for determining that a release has occurred and those who will be affected by it; (5) descriptions of emergency equipment subject to the requirements of the Act; and (6) methods for identifying those responsible for the equipment and facilities, evacuation plans, training programs, and methods and schedules for exercising the plan. Emergency response plans must be made available to the public.

Q. 578.10 When must emergency notification be provided?

Emergency notification must be provided immediately after the release of an extremely hazardous substance occurs. Facilities that use, produce, or store a hazardous chemical must provide emergency notification when (1) the Comprehensive Environmental Response, Corporation, and Liability Act of 1980 (CERCLA) (42 U.S.C. §§9601–9675 (1986)) requires notification of the national response center, (2) the release is not permitted by CERCLA, or (3) the administrator of the EPA determines that notification is required. Notification must also be provided when designated amounts of substances not requiring CERCLA notice are released.

Q. 578.11 Are there any exceptions to the notification requirement?

Yes. Notification is not required when a release results in exposure only to people within the facility's site.

Q. 578.12 Within the meaning of the Emergency Planning and Community Right to Know Act, what is a release?

Within the meaning of the Act, a release occurs when any hazardous chemical, extremely hazardous substance, or toxic chemical is spilled, pumped, poured, emitted, emptied, discharged, injected, leached, dumped, or disposed or leaks or escapes into the environment. Disposal of materials that have first been enclosed in containers is included in the definition.

Q. 578.13 To whom must emergency notification be provided?

Emergency notification must be provided to the community emergency coordinator for the local emergency planning committee of any area likely to be affected by the release and to the state emergency planning commission of any state likely to be affected by the release.

Q. 578.14 What information must emergency notification provide?

Emergency notification must provide information about the nature of the release and the released substance; health risks, medical advice, and precautionary measures relevant to the release; and the name and telephone number of a person to contact for additional information.

Q. 578.15 What reporting requirements are imposed on owners or operators of facilities subject to the requirements of the Emergency Planning and Community Right to Know Act?

The owners or operators of facilities subject to the requirements of the Emergency Planning and Community Right to Know Act must provide MSDSs and emergency and hazardous chemical inventory forms to the appropriate local planning committee, the state emergency response commissions, and the fire departments with jurisdiction over the facilities. Toxic chemical release forms must be provided to the administrator of the EPA and the state official designated by the state's governor.

MSDSs and emergency and hazardous chemical inventory forms provide information about the types, quantities, and location of hazardous chemicals present at the facility. Toxic chemical release forms provide information about the manufacturing, processing, or use of toxic chemicals in excess of the statutorily established threshold amount. Additionally, toxic chemical release forms must provide information about the facility's principal business activities, waste treatment or disposal methods, and the amount of the toxic chemical entering the environment.

Q. 578.16 Does the Emergency Planning and Community Right to Know Act require owners or operators of facilities subject to the requirements of the Act to provide any information directly to members of the public?

Yes. Owners or operators of facilities subject to the requirements of the Act are required to provide the specific chemical identity, if known, of any hazardous or toxic chemical or extremely hazardous substance to any health professional who requests such information in writing, provides a written statement of need (for diagnostic or treatment purposes), and provides a written confidentiality agreement.

Q. 578.17 How may the owner or operator of a facility subject to the requirements of the Act comply with the mandated reporting requirements without disclosing trade secrets?

The specific chemical identity of a hazardous or toxic chemical or an extremely hazardous substance may be withheld if it is established to be a trade secret. In place of the withheld specific chemical identity, the owner or operator must provide the generic class or category of the hazardous or toxic chemical or extremely hazardous substance.

Q. 586 Can an employer legally institute a smoking ban?

Yes. Currently, it appears that employers have the legal right to mandate smoke-free workplaces. The number of employers that ban or limit cigarette smoking on the job has increased steadily in recent years. The Group Against Smoking Pollution, Inc. (GASP) recently released a revised survey of smoking policies imposed by companies and public agencies showing that 148 companies forbid smokers to light up at work, up from 79 companies in 1986. The survey further showed that smoking cigarettes, cigars, or pipes is limited to lounges and cafeteria areas in 107 firms and government agencies, a figure that more than doubled in two years.

An increasing number of workers are affected by smoking bans because of the size of the organizations jumping on the antismoking bandwagon. Among those on the list are the U.S. Department of Health and Human Services, with 120,000 employees; Bell Telephone of Pennsylvania in Philadelphia, with 20,000 employees; Honeywell, Inc., of Minneapolis, with 19,000 workers; and Johns-Manville of Denver, Colorado, and other cities, with 1,000 workers. In addition, public laws banning smoking have supplemented policies of private businesses and have made it more difficult for cigarette smokers to indulge their habit in public.

Q. 587 Is it advisable for a company to mandate a smoke-free workplace?

An outright ban on smoking may appear to be the simplest solution, but it raises some problems. For example, if an employer refuses to hire a smoker, the applicant may claim that he or she is being discriminated against on the basis of a disability, that is, dependence on tobacco. Employers should consult with legal counsel before firing or refusing to hire a smoker.

Negligence-in-employment lawsuits have been brought by nonsmoking employees who assert that an employer has a duty to provide a smoke-free workplace. The success of such claims depends in large part on individual city or county smoking ordinances. Some ordinances, such as the one enacted by New York City, have a $500 maximum penalty per violation. Ordinances of this type are likely to increase the probability of lawsuits by nonsmokers.

Q. 608.1 What is the Drug-Free Workplace Act of 1988?

The Drug-Free Workplace Act of 1988 (Pub. L. No. 100-690) is a federal law that requires federal contractors and federal grant recipients to provide a drug-free workplace or, if they are individuals, to refrain from engaging in unlawful drug-related activities when performing the contract or conducting the grant activity. Federal contractors and federal grant recipients must certify to the contracting or granting agency that they will abide by the requirements of the Act. The provisions of the Act became effective on March 16, 1989. (See Questions 712–728 in this supplement for more information on government contractors.)

Q. 608.2 Who is covered by the Drug-Free Workplace Act of 1988?

Any entity, other than an individual, that desires to be considered a responsible source of government contract supplies, for purposes of being awarded a contract for goods or services in the amount of $25,000 or more, must certify to the contracting agency that it will provide a drug-free workplace.

Q. 608.3 What actions must an employer take to provide a drug-free workplace within the meaning of the Act?

To provide a drug-free workplace within the meaning of the Act, an employer must meet seven requirements. The employer must:

(1) Publish a statement notifying employees that engaging in unlawful drug-related activity is prohibited in the workplace. The statement must also specify what actions will be taken if employees violate the prohibition.

(2) Establish a drug-free awareness program for employees.

(3) Provide each employee engaged in the performance of a government contract or grant with a copy of the published prohibition statement.

(4) Include in the published prohibition statement notice that employment on the government contract or grant is conditioned on the employee abiding by the terms of the statement and notifying the employer within five days of any criminal drug statute conviction for a workplace violation.

(5) Notify the contracting or granting agency within 10 days of receiving notice, from an employee or otherwise, of such a conviction.

(6) Either impose sanctions up to and including termination on any employee who has been convicted for the workplace violation of a criminal drug statute or require that the convicted employee participate in a federal, state, or agency approved drug abuse assistance or rehabilitation program.

(7) Make a good-faith effort to maintain a drug-free workplace.

These requirements apply to federal contractors and federal grant recipients.

Q. 608.4 What constitutes unlawful drug-related activity within the meaning of the Act?

The unlawful manufacture, distribution, dispensing, possession, or use of a controlled substance constitutes unlawful drug-related activity within the meaning of the Act.

Q. 608.5 Must employers make reasonable efforts to provide employees with a drug-free workplace?

The Drug-Free Workplace Act of 1988 requires all federal contractors and federal grant recipients to make a good-faith effort to maintain a drug-free workplace. In so doing, employers must prohibit the unlawful manufacture, distribution, dispensing, possession, and use of controlled substances in the workplace. Employers must also notify employees of the prohibition and of the penalty for violating it, require employees to notify the employer within five days of their criminal conviction for a drug violation occurring in the workplace, and discipline any such employees or require that they attend a drug rehabilitation program. Furthermore, federal contractors and federal grant recipients must certify that they will not unlawfully manufacture, distribute, dispense, possess, or use a controlled substance in the performance of a contract or during the conduct of any activity funded by the grant.

Q. 608.6 What information must a drug-free awareness program provide to employees?

A drug-free awareness program must inform employees about: the dangers of workplace drug abuse; the employer's policy of maintaining a drug-free workplace; drug counseling, rehabilitation, and assistance programs available to employees; and employee penalties for drug abuse violations.

Q. 608.7 What actions may be taken against a federal contractor or federal grant recipient that fails to abide by the drug-free workplace requirement?

Failure to abide by the drug-free workplace requirement may result in the suspension of payments under the contract or grant, termination of the contract or grant, or suspension or debarment of the contractor or grant recipient. These actions are not mutually exclusive; any combination may be taken in response to a single incident. These measures, or any combination thereof, may also be imposed if a contractor or grant recipient provides the contracting or granting agency a false certification, or if the contractor or grant recipient fails to make a good-faith effort to provide a drug-free workplace.

Q. 608.8 What is the effect of debarment?

A federal contractor or grant recipient that has been debarred will be ineligible for the award of any federal agency contract or grant and for participation in any future federal agency contract or grant for a period of up to five years.

Q. 608.9 What will indicate that a federal contractor or grant recipient has failed to make a good-faith effort to provide a drug-free workplace?

If a number of employees of a government contractor or grant recipient are convicted for workplace violations of criminal drug statutes, it may indicate that the contractor or grant recipient has not made the required good-faith effort to provide a drug-free workplace.

Q. 608.10 What special procedures must be followed before measures can be taken against a federal contractor that violates the Drug-Free Workplace Act?

Before measures can be taken against a federal contractor, a contracting officer must make a written determination that cause for action exists. A contracting officer must initiate an appropriate proceeding to determine what, if any, measures should be taken. The contracting agency must conduct the proceeding in accordance with its own procedural rules and those of the federal acquisition regulation. The procedural rules of the federal acquisition regulation are designed to provide a full and fair proceeding. Requirements include the provision of notice and the opportunity to respond in writing or in person. (See Questions 712–728 in this supplement for more on government contractors.)

Q. 608.11 Is there a time limit within which an employer must respond to an employee who has been convicted of a workplace violation of a criminal drug abuse statute?

Yes. An employer must either impose sanctions or require participation in a drug abuse assistance or rehabilitation program within 30 days after receiving notice from an employee of a conviction.

Q. 608.12 Will action always be taken against a federal contractor or grant recipient that has failed to abide by the drug-free workplace requirement, failed to make a good-faith effort, or made a false certification?

No. Action may be waived if the head of the contracting agency determines that taking action would result in severe disruption of the agency to the detriment of the federal government or the public. The head of the granting agency may also waive action if he or she determines that taking action would not be in the public interest.

Q. 608.13 Does the Drug-Free Workplace Act mandate employee drug testing?

No. The Drug-Free Workplace Act does not generally require drug testing of government contractor employees. However, the Department of Defense (DOD) has issued interim regulations that require contractors to establish workplace drug-testing programs or appropriate alternatives. Any drug testing an employer institutes should be only to uncover illegal drug use by employees in sensitive positions (for example, an employee who has been granted access to classified information or whose job the contractor believes to involve national security, health, or safety or that demands a high level of trust and confidence). The contractor may also institute drug testing when it has a reasonable suspicion that an employee uses illegal drugs, when an employee has been involved in an accident or unsafe practice, as part of a follow-up to rehabilitation for past drug use, or as part of a voluntary employee drug-testing program. A contractor is required to follow the DOD regulations if the contract involves access to classified information, the contracting officer determines that the regulations are necessary for protecting national security, health, and so forth, and the contract obligations (or the pertinent part thereof) are to be performed in the United States.

Q. 608.14 Do the provisions of the Drug-Free Workplace Act or the DOD interim rules provide for mandatory penalties for employees who refuse to participate in a drug-testing program?

Neither the Act nor the DOD interim rules require that a contractor penalize an employee for failure to participate in a drug-testing program the contractor institutes. A contractor runs the risk of making a false certification if it does not make a good-faith effort to maintain a drug-free workplace (Question 608.5); this effort may include a notation that certain employees refuse to participate in an otherwise valid drug-testing program.

Q. 608.15 Will mandatory testing of employees or penalties for refusing to participate in a test subject a contractor to a possible lawsuit by an employee?

Several courts have held that mandatory drug testing is a violation of an employee's right of privacy. Some courts also find that random or mandatory drug testing is an unreasonable search and seizure under the Fourth Amendment. However, other courts have held that testing and other searches based on a reasonable, individual, and particularized suspicion are valid and constitutional. Still other courts have found that an employer was liable for intentional infliction of emotional distress, among other things, for firing an employee who refused to participate in a drug test.

Q. 608.16 Are employees who work with video display terminals (VDTs) exposed to special risks?

VDT users have reported repetitive motion injuries, musculoskeletal problems, and eye-focusing problems.

Although employees who work with VDTs are exposed to small

amounts of radiation the VDTs emit, scientific research on the effects of VDT radiation are inconclusive.

Q. 608.17 How can an employer decrease the risks faced by employees who work with VDTs?

An important way employers can decrease the risks faced by employees who work with VDTs is to adjust the work environment. Eye problems can be alleviated by decreasing the illumination in work areas, because overhead fluorescent lighting tends to be very bright compared to a VDT's dark screen. Musculoskeletal problems, including back and neck aches, can be alleviated by using adjustable office equipment, which allows each employee to set his or her chair, keyboard, and screen at a comfortable level. Employers that are concerned about potential radiation exposure problems may want to obtain newer VDTs, which emit less radiation than older models.

Q. 608.18 Does OSHA have any special rules regarding health care workers who may be exposed to the AIDS virus?

In February 1990, the Labor Department's Office of Health Compliance Assistance issued extensive "Enforcement Procedures for Occupational Exposure to Hepatitis B Virus (HBV) and Human Immunodeficiency Virus (HIV)." These procedures apply to OSHA workplace inspections and citations for safety violations. These procedures stem from September 1986, when OSHA received a petition from various labor unions that represented health care employees, to develop standards that would help protect their members from blood-borne diseases. Such standards are still in the developmental stage; according to the Department of Labor, "the Agency has concluded that the risk of contracting hepatitis B and AIDS among members of various occupations within the health care system requires an immediate response through a variety of existing mechanisms."

Q. 608.19 Who are "health care workers" covered by the new OSHA AIDS enforcement procedures?

The new AIDS enforcement procedures apply to virtually all employees of health care facilities, including physicians, dentists and other dental workers, optometrists, podiatrists, chiropractors, laboratory and blood bank technologists and technicians, research laboratory scientists, phlebotomists, dialysis personnel, paramedics, emergency medical technicians, medical examiners, morticians, housekeepers, laundry workers, and others whose work may involve direct contact with body fluids from living individuals or corpses.

Despite this seemingly sweeping definition, the procedures state, just one page later, that "ward clerks and administrators have virtually no increased risk of contact with body fluids (and) are thus at no greater risk of contracting blood-borne diseases than other members of the general population."

Q. 608.20 What sorts of inspections do the new OSHA AIDS procedures call for?

The new procedures modify OSHA's usual inspection practices in a number of ways. First of all, all health service providers (SIC code 80) and funeral homes and crematories (SIC code 7261) from a list, such as Duns Marketing Service, shall be placed in a pool by each OSHA regional administrator. A list of inspection targets will be randomly drawn from the pool. (Establishments with less than 11 employees are excluded.) This list will be narrowed by some additional bureaucratic procedures.

When one of these targeting facilities is visited, the inspector will locate the administrator, medical director, or other person in charge and present his or her appropriate credentials. If the inspector is refused admission, the next step will be to get a search warrant (see Question 549). The inspection will then focus on areas of "primary concern," e.g., emergency rooms, operating rooms, direct patient care areas, laboratories, and x-ray facilities. "Secondary areas" are laundry and housekeeping facilities.

Q. 608.21 What documents will an OSHA inspector want to see during an AIDS inspection?

The OSHA inspector will be particularly interested in the establishments' Infection Control (IC) program and its injury records. An IC program will normally be a written policy "relating to the control of infectious disease hazards where employees may be exposed to direct contact with body fluids." As to recordkeeping, the new OSHA procedure makes the following observation:

> "Needlestick, like any other puncture wound, are considered injuries for recordkeeping purposes due to the instantaneous nature of the event. Only those work-related injuries that involve loss of consciousness, transfer to another job, restriction of work or motion, or medical treatment are required to be put on the OSHA 200 form. Use of prescription medication (beyond a single dose for minor injury or discomfort) is considered medical treatment. Therefore, any needlestick requiring medical treatment, e.g., gamma globulin, hepatitis B immune globulin, hepatitis B vaccine, etc., shall be recorded. In addition, since this type of treatment is considered absolutely necessary, and must be administered by a physician or licensed medical personnel, such an injury cannot be considered minor."

Q. 608.22 What if a facility doesn't have a formal Infection Control program for hepatitis and AIDS?

If there is no written IC Program, the inspector will determine the effectiveness of the facility's program by interviewing employees and inspecting the premises. Even with a formal, written IC Program, it is likely that the inspector will conduct a walk-through examination of the facility and informally interview employees.

Q. 608.23 What will the OSHA inspector's walk-through inspection be like?

During the walk-through examination, the inspector will spot-check various areas of the facility to ensure the Infection Control program is actually in place, is operating as documented, and is effective.

Q. 608.24 Where can an employer get information on the requirements for an acceptable Infection Control program?

The requirements specifically identified by OSHA's February 27, 1990 instructions are found in the Code of Federal Regulations at: 29 C.F.R. 1910.132(a) and (c); 29 C.F.R. 1910.22 (a)(1) and (2); 29 C.F.R. 1910.141(a)(4)(i) and (ii); and 29 C.F.R. 1910.145(F).

29 C.F.R. 1910 is a large volume of OSHA standards, available from local federal bookstores or the U.S. Government Printing Office in Washington, DC.

Depending upon the level of in-house expertise, employers may want to consult legal counsel or an OSHA-oriented consulting firm for additional information on acceptable IC Programs.

Q. 608.25 What is OSHA's citation policy with respect to AIDS and hepatitis inspections?

Citations will normally be issued for violations found in the following areas: personal protective equipment, housekeeping, sanitation and waste disposal, and accident prevention signs and tags.

In addition, health care facilities, like all employers, come under OSHA's general duty to maintain a safe workplace.

Employment Termination

Q. 610 What legal basis might a discharged employee use to assert a claim against an employer?

An employer who believes that his or her employment was wrongfully terminated may file suit against an employer based on such alleged claims as violation of federal or state antidiscrimination or other employee protection statutes, breach of an employment contract, or state common-law exceptions to the at-will doctrine. Liability under any one of these can prove costly to an employer. Even if an employer ultimately avoids liability, the costs incurred in defending such lawsuits can be exorbitant.

The two most often used laws to protect employees are the National Labor Relations Act (NLRA), which prohibits employers from discharging employees for union activities, and Title VII of the 1964 Civil Rights Act, which prohibits terminations based on a person's race, color, religion, sex, or national origin.

Other federal laws containing restrictions on an employer's right to fire workers include:

(1) The Age Discrimination in Employment Act (ADEA)—employers may not discharge workers over 40 years old because of their age.

(2) The Vocational Rehabilitation Act—prohibits federal contractors from discriminating against handicapped workers.

(3) The Fair Labor Standards Act (FLSA)—employers may not discharge employees for exercising their rights guaranteed by minimum wage and overtime provisions of the FLSA.

(4) The Occupational Safety and Health Act (OSHA)—employers may not discharge employees in reprisal for exercising rights under OSHA.

(5) The Employee Retirement Income Security Act (ERISA)—employers cannot discharge employees to prevent them from receiving vested pension benefits.

(6) The Judiciary and Judicial Procedure Act—prohibits employers from discharging workers for serving on a jury.

(7) The Bankruptcy Act—prohibits employers from discharging employees who file for bankruptcy.

(8) The Immigration Reform and Control Act (IRCA)—prohibits employers from discharging employees because of national origin or citizenship.

Q. 611 What are some guidelines employers can follow to avoid wrongful discharge suits?

The following list provides helpful tips employers can follow to avoid lawsuits for wrongful discharge:

(1) It is usually penny wise and pound foolish for an employer to oppose an unemployment insurance claim by a discharged employee.

(2) Do not force or badger a discharged employee into signing a release of any legal claims against the employer.

(3) Resist terminating a long-term employee unless there is evidence of criminal wrongdoing.

(4) Do not violate either the letter or the spirit of company personnel policies.

(5) It is unwise to fire an employee for poor performance unless it can be documented thoroughly and the employee has received prior notice of unsatisfactory performance.

(6) Before terminating an employee, try to get relevant information from more than just the supervisor urging termination.

(7) Do not ignore employee grievances.

(8) Avoid conveying any information regarding the discharge of an employee to others who have no interest in the proceedings.

Only those employees who have a reason to participate in these procedures, such as supervisors or personnel administrators, should be involved in the termination process.

(9) Document all termination actions, and keep this documentation confidential.

Q. 611.1 What are "reasonable termination procedures"?

A generally acknowledged set of reasonable expectations in procedures applicable to both disciplinary and nondisciplinary terminations has evolved in the personnel management area.

Reasonable termination procedures include the following:

(1) Termination should take place early in the week to avoid undue stress and counterproductive behavior.

(2) Termination should be discussed face-to-face and privately. Notifying an employee by mail or memo denies the employee a chance to raise questions regarding the termination. The indirect method of termination may result in added stress, anger, and loss of self-esteem.

(3) Explain the reason for termination.

(4) Allow the employee to remove personal items from a desk, locker, and work area without embarrassment.

(5) Appropriate co-workers and/or customers should be told of the termination directly by the proper management source.

(6) Severance benefits help reduce the pressure and anxiety the employee feels regarding finances.

(7) Prepare letters summarizing severance benefits. This eliminates needless confusion and allows the employee to leave without having to contact the employer again to clarify the severance benefits.

(8) Outplacement assistance may be appropriate but this depends on the reasons for discharge and the size of the employer.

(9) Generally, in terms of references, an employer should provide only titles held and dates of employment.

Q. 611.2 Should employers voluntarily adopt binding arbitration procedures for handling wrongful discharge claims?

Adoption of binding arbitration is an alternative to the time, expense, and risk of substantial damage awards presented during litigation over wrongful discharge claims.

Q. 613.1 What remedies might a court award an employee who has established discriminatory discharge?

Once a court has determined that an employee was the victim of discriminatory discharge or discipline, the court may order:

(1) Reinstatement;

(2) Back pay;

(3) Retroactive seniority;

(4) Monetary damages;

(5) Protective orders; and/or

(6) Attorneys' fees.

Q. 632.1 What roles do personnel managers play in an employee's initial decision to file a lawsuit?

Personnel managers have the best opportunity to forestall litigation at an early stage by providing the plaintiff's lawyers with the other side of the story. This often prevents the discharge from developing into a legal dispute.

The personnel manager's response to an initial inquiry from the plaintiff's attorney is vital because the information the employer provides allows the attorney to evaluate the case and settle at an early stage. But the personnel manager must be discreet and understand the legal issues involved, or he or she should be silent.

From an employer's point of view, the case is never less expensive than during that initial stage when a terminated employee has not yet begun to accrue consequential damages following a discharge.

Q. 632.2 Can an employer fire an employee based solely on a lie detector test?

Even when an employer can legally give a worker a lie detector test under the Employee Polygraph Protection Act of 1988, an adverse employment action cannot be taken solely on the results of that test. There must be some other evidence supporting the decision to terminate or otherwise discipline the tested employee. (See Questions 62.1–62.25.)

Q. 632.3 Can an employer fire an employee because he or she has AIDS?

The Justice Department ruled in a memorandum dated September 27, 1988, that Section 504 of the Vocational Rehabilitation Act of 1973 covers all people with AIDS—and that no justification exists to single out AIDS as a basis for discharge. This new Justice Department opinion supersedes an opinion issued earlier that said that if an employer feared AIDS might be contagious it could lawfully discriminate against the affected individual.

Although the protections under the Vocational Rehabilitation Act are extended to people with AIDS, a federal employer or federally financed program can, in individual circumstances, exclude an AIDS-infected individual from the workplace. If an individual poses a threat to the health and safety of others or is unable to perform his or her job or satisfy the requirement of the program, that individual can be excluded if there is no reasonable way to accommodate these health and safety performance conditions. (See also Questions 219–224 in the main volume.)

Q. 659.1 May an employee sue an employer for wrongful discharge based on the theory that his or her dismissal violated public policy?

Yes. The public policy exception to the employment-at-will doctrine is rapidly expanding to provide greater protection for the large numbers of employees who are considered employees at will.

Q. 659.2 What is "public policy"?

Public policy is generally characterized as a legal requirement that prohibits individuals from acting in any manner that may be harmful to the public or the public good. In determining whether a particular discharge violates public policy, courts examine whether the discharge would violate a person's basic rights, duties, and/or obligations.

Recently, the California courts restricted the public policy interest involved in a wrongful dismissal case by requiring it to be fundamental and substantial as well as distinctly public. (*Foley v. Interactive Data Corp.*, 47 Cal.3d 654 (1988))

Q. 659.3 What *legal rights* might an employee assert that would be protected by the public policy exception?

Although courts differ, generally an employee cannot be discharged for asserting his or her legal right to:

(1) File a workers' compensation claim;

(2) File for bankruptcy;

(3) Assert compensation rights;

(4) Assert stock option rights;

(5) Assert political beliefs;

(6) Refuse to take a lie detector test; or

(7) Vote.

Q. 659.4 What type of employer motives justify an employee's charge that his or her discharge violated public policy?

Generally, employer motives that may support a public policy violation include:

(1) Retaliating against an employee's exercise of a legal right, such as filing a workers' compensation claim;

(2) Penalizing an employee for performing a legal duty, such as jury duty;

(3) Retaliating against an employee for protesting an employer's illegal or unethical activities; or
(4) Penalizing an employee for "blowing the whistle" on improper company activity.

Q. 659.5 What *legal duties* are protected activities under the public policy exception?

Courts have found a public policy interest in protecting employees discharged for reporting for jury duty, fulfilling a military reserve commitment, and obeying a subpoena.

Q. 659.6 In what types of situations might an employee allege he or she was discharged for refusing to commit illegal or unethical acts?

Courts have held that an employer's authority over its employees does not extend to requiring employees to commit criminal acts. Employees will typically raise wrongful discharge claims if they are terminated because they refuse to:

(1) Falsify records;
(2) Commit perjury;
(3) Participate in antitrust price-fixing schemes;
(4) Engage in activity that would endanger the employee's health or safety;
(5) Commit acts that would harm the environment; or
(6) Engage in conduct that would violate professional codes of ethics.

Q. 659.7 Should an employer reinstate a terminated employee?

An employer can attempt to stop the plaintiff/former employee from receiving damages by offering reinstatement after he or she has filed a suit. However, the plaintiff can reject the offer if the workplace would be so hostile that his or her return would be intolerable, he or she would displace another employee, or he or she has already accepted another job.

The employer should be aware, however, that the reinstatement offer could backfire if:

(1) A presumably unsatisfactory former employee accepts the offer to return to his or her old job; or

(2) The plaintiff rejects the offer and the employer has to explain to a court why it offered to rehire an employee who was considered unsuitable a short time earlier.

Q. 659.8 When might a court order reinstatement?

The trial court has discretion to grant reinstatement. The general purpose of reinstatement is to eradicate discrimination. If the employee's former position is no longer available, the court may order the employee to be placed in a comparable position.

Q. 659.9 What noneconomic factors should an employer consider in deciding whether to settle a wrongful discharge suit?

An employer should consider the following factors:

- The demeanor and potential jury appeal of the plaintiff;
- The anticipated testimony and credibility of all probable witnesses;
- The nature of the forum (e.g., jury or nonjury trial, federal or state court, liberal or conservative (usually city or rural) community); and
- The experience and skill of the plaintiff's attorney.

An employer should also consider certain economic factors, including:

- Potential recovery for the plaintiff;
- Whether the plaintiff has found or unsuccessfully attempted to find a new job; and
- Whether the plaintiff may realistically recover punitive damages or an award for pain and suffering.

Q. 679.1 What is "constructive discharge"?

Constructive discharge occurs when an employer causes or allows (see Question 680.2) an employee's working environment to be so difficult or unpleasant that a reasonable person would feel compelled to resign. When conditions are so intolerable that an employee feels forced to resign, the law views the employee as having been fired by the employer.

Q. 680.1 What is "constructive demotion"?

Constructive demotion is similar to constructive discharge. In a constructive demotion situation an employer makes the working conditions so unbearable that a reasonable person in the employee's place would feel compelled to accept a demotion rather than remain in his or her current position.

Q. 680.2 Is an employer liable for intolerable working conditions caused by others?

To hold the employer liable for the hostile environment created by the employee's co-workers or immediate superior, the employee must establish that the employer knew or should have known about the conditions and failed to take appropriate action to remedy the situation. (See Questions 196.1 and 207–208 in this supplement.)

Q. 696 Is there any federal legislation that requires a company to notify the union of its decision to close its operations?

Until very recently, a company was required to give reasonable notice of its decision to close its operations. What constituted "reasonable" notice depended on the circumstances of each case.

Effective February 4, 1989, the Worker Adjustment and Retraining Notification Act (WARN) became law. WARN generally requires employers that are planning a plant closing or mass lay-off to give affected employees at least 60 days' notice of its employment action. (For exceptions to the 60-day notice requirement, see Questions 707–

710 in this supplement.) The Department of Labor (DOL) has recently interpreted WARN and has attempted to clarify some questions that have arisen concerning it.

Q. 697 Has the new federal plant closing law been tested yet?

The first legal action ever to be brought under WARN was filed in April 1989 (little more than two months after WARN's February 4 effective date) by former employees of a New York brokerage house. (*Finnan v. L. F. Rothschild*, No. 89-2718 (S.D. N.Y. 1989) In what is also the first class action suit under WARN, the complaint said that more than 250 employees were laid off without warning. According to the complaint, L. F. Rothschild Holding Co. distributed termination notices on March 10, 1989 that were effective immediately. WARN requires employers of 100 or more people to give 60 days' advance notice. Rothschild claimed that it could not give advance notice because it was seeking funding that might have allowed it to continue operations. WARN does not require a company to provide notice if it is actively seeking capital to prevent or postpone the shutdown. (See Question 708 in this supplement).

Q. 698 Which employers are covered by WARN?

All companies employing 100 or more employees excluding part-time employees, or 100 or more employees including all part-time employees who work in the aggregate at least 4,000 hours per week exclusive of overtime, are covered by WARN whether or not their employees are represented by a union. Employees on temporary lay-off or on leave who have a reasonable expectation of recall are included as employees for purposes of WARN. A worker has a reasonable expectation of recall when he or she is notified, or understands through industry practice, that his or her employment with the company has been only temporarily interrupted and that he or she will be recalled to the same or a similar job.

Q. 699 What constitutes a "plant closing" under WARN?

A plant closing is a permanent or temporary shutdown of a single site of employment, or one or more facilities or operating units within a single site of employment, resulting in 50 or more employees (excluding part-time employees) losing employment during any 30-day period. Any employment action resulting in the effective cessation of production or the work a unit performs, even if a few employees remain, is a shutdown.

Q. 700 What is a "mass lay-off" under WARN?

A mass lay-off is a reduction in workforce that is not due to a plant closing but results in an employment loss at a single site of employment during any 30-day period for at least 33% of the active employees, excluding part-timers, or at least 50 employees, excluding part-timers. If 500 or more full-time employees are affected, notice is required even if that number is less than 33% of the workforce.

The difference between a plant closing and a mass lay-off is that a plant closing involves employment loss resulting from the shutdown of one or more distinct units within a single site or the entire site; a mass lay-off occurs when an employment loss occurs, regardless of whether one or more units at the site are shut down.

Q. 701 Who are "affected employees"?

Affected employees are those employees who may reasonably be expected to lose their jobs as a result of their employer's proposed plant closing or mass lay-off. These employees include individuals who are likely to lose their jobs because of bumping, seniority rights, or other factors, to the extent that these individuals can reasonably be identified at the time the employer is required to give notice. Unlike "employees" within the meaning of the NLRA, "affected employees" under WARN include managerial and supervisory employees. Business partners, consultants, or contract employees who have a separate employment relationship with another employer and are paid by that other employer, or those who are self-employed, are not affected employees under WARN.

Q. 702 What is a "single site of employment"?

The term single site of employment under WARN can refer to either a single location or a group of contiguous locations. Buildings that form a campus or industrial park, or separate facilities across the street from one another, may be considered a single site of employment. Separate buildings or areas that are not directly connected or are not in immediate proximity to one another may be considered a single site of employment if they are in reasonable geographic proximity, are used for the same purpose, and share the same company equipment. An example is an employer that operates several warehouses within an area and transfers and rotates the same employees from one facility to another. When two plants that are managed by a single employer are located on opposite sides of a town, each plant is a separate site if it employs different workers. Similarly, contiguous buildings that are owned by a single employer but that have separate management, produce different products, and employ separate workforces are separate single sites of employment.

Q. 703 Who must give 60 days' notice?

The employer is responsible for designating the most appropriate person within the employer's organization to prepare and serve the required notice.

In the case of the sale of all or part of a business, the seller is responsible for providing notice of any plant closing or mass lay-off that occurs up to and including the effective date of the sale. The buyer must provide notice of any plant closing or mass lay-off that takes place after the date of sale.

If the buyer plans on effecting a plant closing or mass lay-off within 60 days of purchase, the seller may give notice to the affected employees as the buyer's agent. If the seller fails to give notice, the buyer is nevertheless responsible for giving notice. Under these circumstances, buyer and seller should determine the impact of the sale on workers and arrange to give notice to affected employees if they anticipate a mass lay-off or plant closing.

Q. 704 Who must receive notice?

If affected employees are represented by a union, written notice must be served on the union's chief elected officer. If there is no union at the time notice must be given, notice must be served on each affected employee individually. Notice must also be served on the state dislocated worker unit and the chief elected official of the local government within which a closing or lay-off is to occur.

Q. 705 What must the notice contain?

When the affected employees are represented by a union, the notice must contain: (1) the name and address of the employment site at which the closing or lay-off will occur and the name and telephone number of a company official to contact for further information; (2) a statement indicating whether the closing or lay-off is expected to be permanent or temporary and whether the entire plant is to be closed; (3) the schedule for making separations from service, including the anticipated date of the first separation; and (4) the names of the individuals currently holding affected jobs and their job titles.

When the affected employees are not represented by a union, the notice must be written in language employees can understand and must indicate: (1) whether the lay-off will be permanent or temporary and whether the entire plant will be closed; (2) when the plant closing or mass lay-off will commence and the date on which the individual employee will be separated; (3) whether or not employees have bumping rights; and (4) the name and telephone number of a company official to contact for further information.

Finally, the notice that is separately provided to the state dislocated worker unit and to the head of the local government must contain all of the information in the notice to the union or individual employee and, in the case of a union, the name of each union representing affected employees and the name and address of the chief elected officer of each union.

Q. 706 How is the notice served?

The notice may be served in any way that ensures receipt of the notice at least 60 days before the plant closing or mass lay-off. For example, first class mail or personal delivery with optional signed receipt are acceptable methods of delivery. Another viable option, when affected employees must be notified directly, is inserting the notice into pay envelopes.

Q. 707 May notice be given less than 60 days in advance?

WARN's notification period may be less than 60 days in three circumstances: (1) a faltering company; (2) an unforeseeable business circumstance; and (3) a natural disaster.

Q. 708 When is a company a "faltering company" for purposes of WARN?

The faltering company exception to the 60-day notice requirement permits a financially troubled business to avoid the 60-day advance warning if the company is actively seeking financing through any commercially reasonable method with a realistic opportunity of obtaining such financing at the time notice would have been required. This exception applies only to plant closings, not mass lay-offs. The amount of capital or volume of new business sought, if obtained, must be sufficient to have enabled the company to avert or postpone the shutdown.

Because of the fact-intensive nature of the inquiry of what is reasonable or realistic, employers seeking to invoke the faltering company exception under WARN are especially cautioned to consult an attorney to ensure that they are not running afoul of the act.

Q. 709 When does the "unforeseeable business circumstances" exception apply?

Business circumstances that were not reasonably foreseeable at the time that 60-day notice would have been required excuse the employer from the 60-day notice in the case of plant closings and mass lay-offs. An important indication of a business circumstance that is not reasonably foreseeable is a sudden, dramatic, and unexpected action or condition outside the employer's control causing the circumstances. For example, a strike at the employer's major supplier, an important client's unexpected withdrawal from a major contract with the employer, an unexpected and severe economic downturn, and a government-ordered closing of an employment site without prior notice might be considered business circumstances that are not reasonably foreseeable.

Q. 710 When does a "natural disaster" excuse an employer from the 60-day notice requirement?

When a plant closing or mass lay-off is due to a flood, earthquake, drought, storm, tidal wave, or similar natural disaster, advance notice may be precluded. The information stated in the notice, however, must still be given as soon as practicable, whether before or after the occurrence of an employment loss caused by a natural disaster.

The natural disaster exception does not apply when a natural disaster *indirectly* causes a plant closing or mass lay-off. However, the employer may be able to avail itself of the unforeseeable business circumstance exception.

Q. 711 What is an employer's liability if it fails to give the required notice under WARN?

In the event of a plant closing or mass lay-off, an employer that fails to give the required notice under WARN may be assessed back pay for each affected employee for each day of violation, up to a maximum of 60 days. The employer is further liable for the cost of employee benefits for each day of violation.

When an employer fails to provide the required notice to the local government, it is subject to a civil penalty of up to $500 for each day of violation.

Q. 711.1 Can firing an employee on the basis of a positive drug test give rise to a wrongful discharge suit?

The "war on drugs" has resulted in the proliferation of drug tests in American companies. Government contractors are required to maintain drug-free workplaces. Many federal, state, and local agencies, especially those involved with public safety or transportation, have embraced various types of testing, too. Some private employers, though not required by law to test, have chosen to do so, at least under some limited circumstances. Not surprisingly, much of this testing has resulted in litigation. Most cases have been directed at government agencies by their employees or the unions that represent them.

However, there have been a few private civil actions reported. In Pennsylvania, the mid-level appellate court ruled in June 1989 that an employer did not violate any clear mandate of public policy by terminating an employee who had tested positive on a drug screening, the results of which were not reconfirmed by a second drug test. Therefore, the termination did not amount to an exception to the employment-at-will rule. In New York, however, an investment banker has been permitted to proceed with his suit against Bear Sterns, in which he alleges that a positive drug test was the result of blood-level traces of poppy-seed rolls he had eaten, instead of narcotics in his bloodstream. (See *ABA Journal*, July 1990.)

Government Contractors

Q. 712 On what grounds may a contractor be debarred or suspended from performing government contracts?

The government may debar a contractor if the contractor is convicted of fraud or a criminal offense in connection with obtaining or attempting to obtain a contract, for embezzlement, for any offense indicating a lack of business integrity or honesty, or for violation of the terms of a contract such as a willful failure to perform or a history of failure to perform. A contractor will be held liable for an employee's acts of criminal fraud or other acts justifying debarment or other penalties if the contractor in any way encouraged or condoned the employee's acts.

(See also Questions 608.1–608.15 for information about the Drug-Free Workplace Act.)

Q. 713 What steps must a contractor take to protect classified information that it obtains pursuant to bidding for a contract or in performing a contract for the Department of Defense?

A contractor is required to follow numerous steps to protect classified information, including appointing a U.S. citizen to direct and supervise appropriate security measures, limiting the disclosure of information to authorized persons only, providing suitable methods for safeguarding classified information, performing security checks within its facility, and providing limited access to restricted areas. The extensive list of duties the contractor is required to perform is set forth in the Industrial Security Manual for Safeguarding Classified Information, published by the Department of Defense. Employees who are noncitizens are generally restricted from access to classified information.

Q. 714 Is it sufficient for a contractor to certify that it has complied with or will comply with the Industrial Security Manual for Safeguarding Classified Information?

No. The manual requires a contractor to establish a standard practice and procedure for implementing the safeguards explained in the manual. Employees should be educated regarding retention and destruction of classified materials, handling and transfer of classified materials, and methods for internal and external reporting of unauthorized divulgence of information.

Q. 715 What are the basic requirements for security clearance for a contractor's employees?

Generally, only U.S. citizens can be granted a standard security clearance. A naturalized U.S. citizen whose country of origin is determined to have interests adverse to the United States must have been a U.S. citizen for five years or have resided in the United States for the past 10 years. To be cleared for confidential information, an individual must be at least 16 years old; to be cleared for secret or top secret information, an individual must be at least 18 years old; and any non–U.S. citizens must be at least 21 years old to be cleared for secret or top secret information.

Q. 716 Who grants security clearances?

Clearances for top secret, secret, or sensitive information or restricted data are granted solely by the Department of Defense. A contractor may grant a clearance for confidential information only.

Q. 717 May immigrants be granted security clearances?

Generally, security clearances are limited to U.S. citizens. However, an immigrant alien may be granted a limited access authorization if (1) his or her access is limited to a specific government contract; (2) he or she possesses a rare or unusual expertise; (3) a qualified U.S. citizen cannot be hired in sufficient time to meet the contractual requirement the individual will fulfill; and (4) he or she resides permanently in the U.S., has a green card, and certifies his or her intent to become a U.S. citizen as soon as possible.

Q. 718 Is a government contractor required to provide equal opportunity programs?

Procuring agencies must include in all contracts a clause requiring the contractor to certify whether or not it has established an affirmative action program at its facilities. Exemptions to the requirement may be made for contracts that the contracting agency determines to be essential to national security, contracts for goods or services totaling less than $10,000 in value, contracts for work outside of the United States, contracts with state or local governments, or other contracts that the director of the office of federal contract compliance programs determines to be subject to special circumstances that justify exemption.

Q. 719 What sanctions may a contractor suffer for failure to comply with equal opportunity requirements?

The contract may be canceled, terminated, or suspended for failure to comply with the government's equal opportunity requirements. Further, the contractor's name may appear in a public listing of "nonawardable prospective contractors," which is tantamount to a suspension or debarment from performing government contracts.

Q. 719.1 Which government agency enforces equal opportunity programs with government contractors?

Like most employers in America, government contractors are subject to the Equal Employment Opportunity Commission's jurisdiction. But in addition to the EEOC, the Office of Federal Contract Compliance Programs (OFCCP) in the Labor Department is charged with insuring that contractors comply with their affirmative action requirements. A disappointed employee or job applicant not only can file a discrimination charge with EEOC, but also can complain to OFCCP, which may then step in and review the contractor's entire affirmative action program. It is questionable, however, whether or not the OFCCP vigorously investigates such complaints; the OFCCP has been cited for failure to adequately perform its investigative duties.

Perhaps in response to such political heat, OFCCP in 1990 struck out in some new enforcement directions. According to an announcement by Deputy Director Leonard Biermann last March, the agency's "glass ceiling initiative" will focus for the first time on succession plans within corporate contractors, i.e., how these companies choose the people who fill high-level executive jobs. Interest appears to be focused primarily on Fortune 500 companies.

On the litigation front, OFCCP has shifted emphasis from handicap discrimination cases to Executive Order 11246, the original John F. Kennedy presidential proclamation mandating affirmative action by government contractors.

Q. 720 May a government contractor's employees be required to work for less than the prevailing minimum wage?

No. Under the Walsh-Healey Act, a contractor may not pay an employee less than the prevailing minimum wage, even if the employee is willing to agree to a lower rate of pay.

Q. 721 What is the Davis-Bacon Act?

The Davis-Bacon Act requires contracts exceeding $2,000 in value to set forth the minimum wages to be paid to all classes of laborers a contractor employs in the performance of the contract. Contractors and subcontractors must agree to pay their employees no less than the stated minimum rates.

Q. 722 May a government contractor recover the costs of recruiting and training employees?

Pursuant to restrictions set forth in the federal acquisition regulations, a contractor may charge against a contract recruitment costs, including educational testing programs and travel and relocation costs connected with recruiting new employees. Also subject to restrictions, the contractor may charge the government for the costs of training and educating employees, including those incurred for materials, textbooks, tuition, and fees.

Q. 723 Should a contractor require its employees to report infractions of time charging or other cost accounting rules and regulations?

Yes. Government contractors are held accountable for failures to accurately charge the government for time employees spend on government contracts. Accordingly, a mischarging of time by an employee or a number of employees to a contract on which they have not actually worked is considered a serious infraction. A contractor should therefore educate employees about the importance of correctly charging their time to contracts on which they have worked, preventing inadvertent or intentional mischarging of time, reporting infractions of time charging rules and regulations both internally and externally, auditing accounting records to determine whether contracts have been accurately and appropriately charged, and reporting to the government any infractions with recommendations for corrective and/or restitutional actions.

Q. 724 Will the commission of a crime or an infraction by an individual employee automatically subject a contractor to debarment or other penalties?

No. Although the government may seek to prosecute the corporation if it believes that the wrongful act was a result of or was otherwise condoned by the corporation's lack of internal controls, education, and efforts at compliance, the government may also seek to prosecute only an individual employee for his or her wrongful acts. Thus, an individual employee who is acting in contravention of the company's established policy and without the company's knowledge may be subject to individual prosecution for his or her wrongful acts.

Q. 725 May a contractor charge the government for employee wage rates that are beyond those charged to commercial customers?

No. Discriminatory pricing against the government is forbidden, and costs that include greater compensation payments to employees than they would be paid for nongovernment work are prohibited. Further, fringe benefits such as insurance premiums and holiday pay are not direct costs of a particular contract; they are overhead costs that are negotiated separately under the contract. Overhead may include the cost of providing employee morale, health, and welfare activities (e.g., first aid classes or income tax information).

Q. 726 Are contractors required to inform the government if they have used consultants to aid in obtaining government contracts?

Yes. The federal acquisition regulations require a contractor to report to the government any arrangement it makes with a nonemployee individual (or entity) whereby the individual obtains or solicits a contract and is paid contingent on success. When the contractor provides a guarantee that it has not employed any such individual or entity, a breach of the guarantee may result in contract annulment or deduction from the contract price of any contingent fee paid.

Q. 727 What restrictions are placed on the hiring of former government employees by government contractors?

A former government employee a contractor hires is forbidden by federal criminal law to represent the contractor in regard to any judicial proceeding or to attempt to obtain a contract or pursue another particular matter in which he or she participated personally while a government employee. Further, a former government employee will commit a criminal act if, within two years after being employed by the government, he or she represents a government contractor before the U.S. government to obtain a contract, ruling, or determination if such a determination pertains to a matter that was actually pending under his or her official responsibility as a government employee within one year prior to his or her termination or in which he or she participated personally as a government officer or employee. The prohibition also extends to partners of the former government employee and carries with it substantial criminal penalties. However, the law does not prohibit a former government employee from performing certain acts on behalf of the contractor, such as giving testimony or furnishing scientific or technological information under procedures that the particular government agency considers acceptable. In addition, a recent regulation requires that the contractor certify that it has not offered employment or inducement to a government employee in return for a contract or otherwise sought source selection or proprietary information.

Q. 728 What other labor restrictions apply to government contractors?

Under the Walsh-Healey Act, contractors may not employ children or convicts in the performance of government contracts. Children are defined in the federal acquisition regulations as persons under 16 years of age. Convicts do not include those persons convicted but on parole or otherwise discharged from prison. A contractor must also maintain and make available for inspection employment records listing the name, address, sex, and occupation of each employee as well as wage and employment records for each employee. A contractor must stipulate that the performance of the contract for the government does not entail working conditions that are unsanitary or hazardous to the health and safety of employees. Contractors may satisfy the working conditions requirement by showing compliance with the health and safety laws of the state in which the contract is performed.

(See also Questions 608.1–608.15.)

Appendix A

CONGRESSIONAL ACTIVITY 1989—1990 (through June 15, 1990)

PLANT CLOSINGS

S. 2527–Plant Closing Notification Bill

This law became effective on February 4, 1989. (See Questions 696–711.)

POLYGRAPH TESTING

H.R. 1212—The Employee Polygraph Protection Act

This law became effective on June 27, 1988. (See Questions 62.1–62.25.)

WHISTLEBLOWERS

S. 436—Employee Health and Safety Whistleblower Protection Act

Although not enacted, similar legislation passed on April 10, 1989 (the Whistleblower Protection Act of 1989, Pub. L. No. 101-12

(103 Stat. 16)). On April 26, 1990, a Senate panel approved a substitute version of this bill.

HANDICAP DISCRIMINATION

S. 933/H.R. 2273—The Americans With Disabilities Act

Bills passed in both houses in 1990. (See Appendix B.)

AIDS DISCRIMINATION

S. 933/H.R. 2273—The Americans With Disabilities Act

On June 25, 1990, a House-Senate conference committee narrowly defeated a controversial amendment to allow transfer of HIV-positive employees out of food-handling positions.

EQUAL EMPLOYMENT OPPORTUNITY

S. 2104/H.R. 4000—Civil Rights Act of 1990

As of June 18, 1990, the White House reportedly was drafting compromise amendments to modify the three most controversial provisions. A bill may reach the Senate floor before the July 4 recess. (See Appendix B.)

STRIKE REPLACEMENTS

S. 2112/H.R. 3936—A Bill to Amend the National Labor Relations Act

In June 1990, Congress had still not acted on these bills. Meanwhile, former Labor Secretaries Marshall and Wirtz joined a group of other prominent leaders to form a Committee for Workplace Fairness to support the bills.

FAMILY AND MEDICAL LEAVE

H.R. 770—Family and Medical Leave Act

Passed by the Senate on June 18, 1990, but President Bush threatened a veto. (See Appendix B.)

HATCH ACT REFORM

S. 135/H.R. 20—Hatch Act amendments

In May and June 1990, proposed amendments were introduced in both houses, aimed at easing restrictions on federal employees' political activities.

CHILD CARE

H.R. 3/S. 5.5—Act for Better Child Care

If H.R. 3 passes in the House in 1990, it will permit limited use of flexible spending accounts for tax-deductible child care expenses of workers.

CLEAN AIR

H.R. 3030/S.1630—Clean Air Act Reauthorization

The Senate version includes amendments on asbestos, industrial accidents, and cooperation between OSHA and the Chemical Safety Board.

On May 23, 1990, the House approved an amendment to extend unemployment insurance and provide retraining for workers affected by the Act.

EMPLOYEE TERMINATION

No bill is before the Congress at present. However, the National Conference of Commissioners on Uniform State Laws continues to work on a Uniform Employment Termination Act. Additionally, National Labor Relations Board Chairman Edward B. Miller has proposed an amendment to the National Labor Relations Act that would make an unjust discharge an unfair labor practice.

HEALTH AND SAFETY

H.R. 4652/S.930—Construction Safety, Health, and Education Improvement Act

Bill aims to improve safety in the construction industry. Organized labor has endorsed the bill; OSHA and the construction industry say administrative changes are preferable to the passage of a new law.

H.R. 3521—Nuclear Facilities Occupational Safety Improvement Act

OSHA and the Energy Department told a House panel in June 1990 that extension of OSHA authority into Department of Energy nuclear weapons plants, per this bill, is unnecessary for worker health and safety.

S. 2154—OSHA Criminal Penalty Perform Act

Bill would strengthen the criminal penalties currently called for under OSHA.

S. 2442—Occupational Safety and Health Hazards Victims Rights Act

Bill introduced by Senator Paul Simon of Illinois in April 1990 would amend OSHA to allow injured workers or surviving family members to take part in OSHA investigations.

CHILD LABOR

S. 2548—Child Labor Act of 1990

Introduced by Senator Metzenbaum of Ohio, this bill seems to be an attempt to "ride the bandwagon" of current concern for teen labor in fast-food and other industries.

Appendix B

PENDING LEGISLATION 1990—1991

THE CIVIL RIGHTS ACT OF 1990

This Act has been proposed principally in response to the Supreme Court's *Wards Cove* decision (see Questions 191 and 191.1). It would restore the use of statistics to their pre-*Wards Cove* position of power in proving job discrimination by means of the "disparate impact" test.

A neutral employment policy can be held to have a disparate impact on a minority group, even though there is no evidence of intentional discrimination, if statistics show an imbalance between the make-up of the Company's workforce and the labor pool at large. *Wards Cove* made the burden of proving such a case, absent evidence of an employer's improper motive, much more difficult for plaintiffs. Not every civil rights advocate wants to see *Wards Cove* legislatively reversed. For instance, journalist Thomas Sewell wrote in the June 5, 1990 issue of the Philadelphia *Daily News*, "Nowhere are issues more misstated than in the Civil Rights Act of 1990 being debated in Congress. . . . Lawyers will be the biggest gainers because the bill makes it possible to sue an employer for discrimination even if there is not a living soul with any evidence that he or she was personally discriminated against."

Additionally, Section 8 of the proposed law would allow an alleged victim of intentional bias to claim compensatory and punitive damages in addition to back pay. Such a remedy is already available under the old (post-Civil War) civil rights acts, known as Sections

1981 and 1983. Groups such as the Women Employed Institute are urging adoption of Section 8 to offset the threats of harassment and blacklisting that they claim discourage suits today.

FAMILY AND MEDICAL LEAVE ACT

As of June 1990, the Bush Administration was still vociferous in its opposition to mandated parental leave. Although the Administration "supports and encourages parental and medical leave policies," says a June 17 statement from the Office of Management and Budget, "this objective can be best achieved voluntarily through employee–employer negotiations or the normal collective bargaining process between management and labor, not by the federal government mandating employee benefits."

The parental leave issue came to public attention some three years ago when the Supreme Court ruled that California's parental leave law was constitutional. Since then, other states have enacted similar legislation (see Question 406.12). Many companies, across the country and across all industries, have adopted some sort of maternity or parental leave policy in their employee handbooks—more or less in line with OMB's recommendation that this employee benefit be instituted at the grass-roots level.

Appendix C

AMERICANS WITH DISABILITIES ACT

OVERVIEW

On July 26, 1990, President George Bush signed into law the Americans with Disabilities Act (ADA). Generally, the law prohibits discrimination against people with disabilities in the areas of employment, public service (including transportation), public accommodations, and telecommunication services. The ADA also contains a miscellaneous section that addresses attorneys' fees, illegal drug use, and amendments to the Rehabilitation Act of 1973. Title I of the ADA prohibits discrimination in employment activities against a qualified person with a disability. Title I borrows much of its procedural framework from Title VII of the Civil Rights Act of 1964 by incorporating Title VII's enforcement, notice posting, and employer coverage provisions. The underlying premise of Title I is that persons with disabilities should not be excluded from job opportunities unless they are actually unable to do the job.

DEFINITIONS

The key terms defined in Section 101 of the ADA are *disability*, *employer*, *reasonable accommodation*, and *undue hardship*.

Disability. An individual with a disability is defined as someone who has a physical or mental impairment that substantially limits one or more major life activities, or as someone who is regarded as having such an impairment. Thus, a cured cancer victim or an individual with a disfiguring scar, for example, may be disabled if that person is regarded by others as disabled. In order to be protected under the ADA, the individual must fall within the meaning of a "qualified individual with a disability," which is an individual with a disability who, with or without reasonable accommodation, can perform the essential functions of the job. "Essential functions" are job tasks that are fundamental and not marginal to job performance. The Committee on Education and Labor points out that the "inclusion of this phrase ["essential functions"] is useful in emphasizing that handicapped persons should not be disqualified simply because they may have difficulty in performing tasks that bear only a marginal relationship to a particular job."

Employer. Under the ADA, an employer is a person or persons engaged in industry affecting commerce who has 15 or more employees for each working day in each of 20 or more calendar weeks in the current or preceding calendar year. However, the United States government, corporations wholly owned by the U.S. government, Indian tribes, and private membership clubs are specifically excluded from this definition.

Reasonable Accommodation. "Reasonable accommodation" incorporates a range of actions that may be necessary to allow a person with a disability to perform the essential functions of a job. For example, reasonable accommodation actions include, but are not limited to, job restructuring; allowing part-time or modified work schedules; making existing facilities readily accessible to and usable by individuals with disabilities; reassigning employee to a vacant position; acquiring or modifying equipment or devices; adjusting or modifying examinations, training materials, policies; providing qualified readers for the visually impaired or interpreters for the hearing impair and other similar accommodations.

The employer must make reasonable accommodations regarding not only hiring and promotion practices, but also the full gamut of employment decisions (promotions, transfers, wages, etc.).

According to the Committee on Education and Labor, employers should not assume that accommodations are required without consulting the applicant or employee with the disability. Stereotypes about disability can result in stereotypes about the need for accommodations, thereby exceeding what may be actually required. The employee or applicant is responsible for requesting a reasonable accommodation, and the employer will not be liable for failing to provide an accommodation if the employee or applicant does not request it. Conversely, an employer may be liable if it provides an accommodation that could have an adverse impact on an individual.

Despite the ADA's reasonable accommodation requirement, an employer is not obligated to provide any type of assistance if it would impose an "undue hardship."

Undue Hardship. Factors determining whether a reasonable accommodation would pose an undue hardship on an employer include (a) the overall size of the business, (b) the site involved, and (c) the nature and cost of the accommodation needed. Additionally, the number of employees or applicants potentially benefitting from an accommodation may be a relevant consideration in determining undue hardship. Another factor that may be considered in determining undue hardship is the availability of outside funding (from state vocational rehabilitation agencies or from Federal, state, or local tax deductions or credits) to pay for accommodations.

The type of business operation also affects whether or not an accommodation imposes an undue hardship. For example, to implement or maintain physical accessibility for a job applicant or employee who uses a wheelchair might fundamentally alter the nature of the construction site or be unduly costly if the site's terrain and building structure changes daily as construction progresses.

The determination of undue hardship is made on a case-by-case basis. The burden is on the employer to demonstrate that the needed accommodation would cause an undue hardship.

According to the Committee on Education and Labor, the definition of undue hardship intends to discourage an employer who would, for example, otherwise elect to close a store that is only marginally profitable, rather than to undertake significant investments to make reasonable accommodations for employees with disabilities. The requirements of the ADA should not result in the closure of a business or in the loss of jobs.

By including a number of factors to consider, the ADA intends to establish a flexible approach in determining undue hardship.

DISCRIMINATION

Discrimination against a qualified individual with a disability is prohibited in all parts of the employment process. The employment process specifically includes, but is not limited to, job application procedures, hiring, advancement, discharge, compensation, job training, recruitment and advertising, job assignments, job classifications, organizational structures, position descriptions, lines of progression, seniority lists, leaves of absence, sick leave, fringe benefits available by virtue of employment whether or not administered by the employer, employer-sponsored activities (including social or recreational programs), and other terms, conditions, and privileges of employment.

Employers can, however, continue to use job-related criteria in choosing qualified employees. For example, for a job that requires the lifting of 50-pound boxes, the employer may test applicants and employees to determine whether or not they can lift 50-pound boxes. Similarly, an employer can continue to give typists tests to determine their typing skills.

Section 102(b)(1) of the ADA prohibits the employer from limiting, segregating, or classifying a job applicant or an employee in a way that adversely affects the opportunities or status of the applicant or employee based on that person's disability. Therefore, an employer could not adopt a different pay scale, benefits program, promotion opportunities, or working area for employees with disabilities.

Contractual Relationships. Section 102(b)(2) of Title I provides that a covered entity, i.e., a business subject to the ADA, may not participate in a contractual relationship that has the effect of subjecting qualified applicants or employees to discrimination. An employer cannot, therefore, enter into a contractual relationship with another company that would have the effect of discriminating against the employer's own employees or applicants. For example, assume that ABC Corporation is seeking to contract with XYZ Company to provide training for ABC's employees. Whatever responsibilities of accommodation that would apply to ABC Corporation if it provided the training itself would also apply in the contractual relationship. Thus, if XYZ Company was planning to hold its training program in a location that was inaccessible to ABC's employees with disabilities, ABC Corporation would have a duty to consider various reasonable accommodations, including asking the training company to identify other sites for the program that would be accessible, identifying other training companies that use accessible sites, paying to have the training company train the disabled employee (either on a one-to-one basis or with other employees who may have missed the training for other reasons), or any other accommodation that might result in making the training program available to the employee.

Furthermore, the employer has an affirmative duty to investigate the accessibility of an off-site location that it plans to use for its own employees. In such situations, an employer can protect itself by simply insuring that the contract with the host facility specifies that the rooms that are to be used for the function (including meeting rooms, exhibit halls, sleeping rooms, and dining facilities) are accessible in accordance with applicable standards. If the facility breaches this accessibility provision, it will be liable to the employer for the cost of any accommodation needed to provide access to the disabled individual during the off-site function.

Common Administrative Control. Section 102(b)(3) of the ADA prohibits employers from using standards, criteria, or methods of administration that have the effect of discrimination or that perpetuate discrimination by others who are subject to common administrative control. For example, an employer could not enter into a contract for liability insurance with an insurance company who refused to cover accidents or injuries of persons with disabilities. Nor could the employer refuse to hire a person with a disability because its liability policy did not cover persons with disabilities.

Association with Persons with a Disability. Under Section 102(b)(4) of the ADA, an employer cannot discriminate against an employee or an applicant who associates with a person with a disability because of that association. These associations may include family, friends, and people who provide care for persons with disabilities.

This provision applies only when the employer knows of the association with the disabled person and knows of the disability. The burden of proof is on the individual who is claiming discrimination; he or she must prove that the discrimination was motivated by his or her relationship or association with a person with a disability. Therefore, it would be a violation of Title I for an employer to discriminate against a qualified employee who did volunteer work for persons with AIDS, if the employer knew of the employee's relationship or association with the persons with AIDS or the volunteer organization *and* if the employment action was motivated by that relationship or association. Further, it would be illegal for an employer to discriminate against a qualified employee because that employee had a family member or friend who had a disability, if the employer knew about the relationship and acted on that basis.

Qualification Standards. Section 102(b)(6) prohibits the use of qualification standards, employment tests, or other selection criteria that screen out or tend to screen out persons with disabilities, unless the criteria is shown to be job related and consistent with business necessity. The intent is that employment-related tests actually measure what they report to measure. Thus, it would be discriminatory to administer speaking and listening skills to a person with a disability that impairs speech and hearing if the essential functions of the job do not require those skills.

A qualification standard may include a requirement that an individual not pose a direct threat to the health and safety of others. A "direct threat" is defined as a significant risk to the health and safety of others that cannot be eliminated by reasonable accommodation. The Committee on Labor and Education notes that the definition and standard apply not only to those with contagious diseases or infections, but also to individuals with disabilities.

ADA's goal is to eliminate instances in which a person with a disability is excluded or found to be unqualified, based on stereotypes or fear. Therefore, the Act prohibits employment decisions based on generalizations about a disability rather than on the facts of an individual case. For example, an employer may not assume that a person with a mental disability or a person who has been treated for a mental disability poses a direct threat to others. In such instances, there must be objective evidence that the person has a recent history of committing overt acts of making threats that caused harm or that directly threatened harm. The determination of a significant risk must be based on the *current* condition of the applicant or employee. The decision to exclude cannot be based simply on "an elevated risk injury."

Pre-employment Medical Examinations and Inquiries. The ADA provides that an employer may conduct a medical examination or make inquiries as to whether an applicant has a disability or as to the nature or severity of the disability. However, the employer may make pre-employment inquiries only as to the ability of an applicant to perform job-related functions. After an offer of employment has been made, an employer may require a medical examination and may condition the offer of employment on the results of the examination. However, all employees entering within the same employment category must be subject to the same examination. The results of this test, including the medical report and history of the applicant, must be collected and maintained on separate forms and kept in separate files from general personnel information.

According to the Committee on Education and Labor, the Act does not override any legitimate medical standards or requirements established by federal, state, or local laws or by employers for applicants for safety or security-sensitive positions, if the medical standards are consistent with the Act.

Medical Examinations and Inquiries During Employment. An employer may conduct voluntary medical examinations that are part of an employee health program available to all employees at a particular work site. The ADA, therefore, does not prohibit the continuation of voluntary "corporate wellness" programs.

There are several instances in which an employer may inquire into the nature or severity of a disability of a qualified individual without being subject to the penalties of the Act. Such circumstances include (1) when an employer is taking voluntary action to overcome the effects or conditions that will result in long-term opportunities for persons with disabilities, (2) when an employer is taking remedial action to correct the effects of past discrimination, or (3) when an employer is taking affirmative action required by Section 503 of the Rehabilitation Act of 1973. Under any of these circumstances, the inquiring employer must make clear that the information requested is intended for use solely in connection with its remedial actions, obligations, or its voluntary or affirmative action efforts and that the information should be furnished on a purely voluntary basis.

ILLEGAL DRUG USE AND TESTING (SECTION 104)

Illegal Use. Section 104(a) of the ADA provides that "a qualified individual with a disability" does not include an employee or applicant who is a current user of illegal drugs. However, Section 104(b) provides that rehabilitated individuals and those in treatment who no longer use illegal drugs and individuals who are erroneously regarded as illegal drug users are not excluded from the definition of an "individual with a disability." As in all other disability cases, the employee must prove that he or she has a history of a disability or is regarded as having a disability in order to be protected by the ADA.

Drug Testing. Under the Act, employers may test their employees for the use of illegal drugs. An employer may terminate or refuse to hire someone whose test indicates the presence of an illegal substance. However, it would be a violation of the Act to discriminate on the basis of prescription drugs taken by individuals with disabilities who are under the care and supervision of a licensed health care professional.

ENFORCEMENT

Title I of the ADA incorporated the powers, remedies, and procedures set forth in the Civil Rights Act of 1964. The Equal Employment Opportunity Commission has been designated as the enforcement agency for the ADA. The Act provides that the powers and procedures available to persons discriminated against based on disability be the same as, and parallel to, those available to persons discriminated against based on race, color, religion, sex, or national origin. For employers that have 25 or more employees, Title I becomes effective two years after its enactment; for employers with 15 or more employees, the ADA becomes effective four years after its enactment.

SUMMARY

The ADA is a collection of far-reaching provisions that attempt to provide a clear and comprehensive national mandate to end discrimination against individuals with disabilities, to bring such persons into the economic and social mainstream of American life, and to provide enforceable standards that address discrimination against individuals with disabilities.

Title I of the ADA pursues the anti-discrimination mandate in the area of employment. In addition to prohibiting discrimination in employment against individuals with disabilities, Title I incorporates many of the standards of discrimination established in Section 504 of the Rehabilitation Act of 1973, including the obligation to furnish reasonable accommodations for persons with disabilities, unless those accommodations would cause an undue hardship to the employer.

Index

(References in the index are to question numbers in either the main volume or the supplement. Use the supplement, rather than the main volume, if an "S" follows a question number.)

- N -

- O -

- T -

- U -

- V -

- W -